STAY IN THE FIGHT

THE STORY OF THE WORLD CHAMPION WASHINGTON NATIONALS

Josh Crutchmer, *Cover Design*
Nicky Brillowski, *Book Design*

ISBN: 978-1-940056-76-0 (HC)
978-1-940056-78-4 (PB)

Printed in the United States of America
KCI Sports Publishing   3340 Whiting Avenue, Suite 5   Stevens Point, WI 54481
Phone: 1-800-697-3756   Fax: 715-344-2668
www.kcisports.com

Contents

UNFORGETTABLE

Washington Nationals — World Champions!

Sounds pretty good doesn't it? Fans in Washington D.C. have waited an awfully long time to utter those words, and finally, the Nationals are on top.

Let the celebration begin!

It is an honor to write an introduction to such a historic season. It's not easy to win in the big leagues and it is even more difficult to do so in the playoffs when you're playing against the very best every night. But this Nationals team stayed in the fight and found a way to win. How about the come from behind win over Milwaukee in the Wild Card? Or Howie Kendrick's grand slam that knocked off the Dodgers in Game 5 of the NLDS? And, of course, the incredible come from behind Game 7 win to clinch the World Series.

In the following pages we proudly bring you on a trip down memory lane of this championship season that came to its jubilant conclusion in Houston. Stay In The Fight provides Nationals fans the best view in the house of all the ups and downs of the season and gives you an inside look at the incredible World Series win against a very talented Houston Astros team that gave new meaning to the term "road warriors."

Our heartfelt congratulations go out to Ted and Mark Lerner, General Manager Mike Rizzo, Manager Dave Martinez and his staff, and the entire Nationals team on their accomplishments this season. Celebrate this season Washington fans, and save this book to revisit the Nationals' magical moments and unforgettable team — both stars and role players — who rewarded your faith with a World Championship.

Congratulations Washington Nationals! Let's do it again soon.

KCI Sports Publishing

The Washington Nationals celebrate after winning Game 7 of the World Series.

Pitching Expected to Take Nats Far in 2019

You can't talk about the 2019 outlook for the Washington Nationals without first addressing the elephant on the field — mainly that franchise icon Bryce Harper has departed to Philadelphia thanks to a record-setting, 13-year, $330 million contract. But even without the former MVP at Nats Park, the team is still flush with outstanding talent and has made some of the savviest moves of the offseason.

The team signed Patrick Corbin, the top pitcher on the free agent market, to a six-year, $140 million contract in early December. Coming off a season in which he went 11-7 with a 3.15 ERA, striking out 246 batters in 200 innings pitched, the former Arizona Diamondback immediately made the already formidable rotation arguably the best in baseball.

"I think [the Nationals] have won the most games in regular season baseball in the last five [or] six years," Corbin says. "And knowing how deep of a team they are, I saw this as a place that I could live for a long time and be part of this rotation. Being a new guy here, it seems like it's been easy to join and be part of it."

Staff ace Max Scherzer struck out 300 batters in 220 innings on his way to a league-leading 18 wins and 2.53 ERA. While Stephen Strasburg had some injury concerns last year, he still managed 10 wins and 156 Ks in just 130 innings; he's looked healthy all spring and should be poised for a top season. The rest of the rotation includes veterans Aníbal Sánchez and Jeremy Hellickson — both recent free agent signees — and 25-year-old Joe Ross, who has been a dependable arm for the Nats since 2015 as insurance against injury.

Sean Doolittle established himself nicely at the closer in 2018, as the lefty recorded 25 saves and an anemic 1.60 ERA. This year, he's joined in a revamped pen by veteran Trevor Rosenthal, who will serve as his primary setup man, as well as young fireballers Kyle Barraclough, Koda Glover and Justin Miller. The new additions reinforce a bullpen that should improve on its overall 4.05 ERA.

Even without Harper, the Nats shouldn't have any problems scoring runs. A breakout season by rookie Juan Soto last year is just the tip of the iceberg of what MLB experts expect from the left fielder. Expect plenty of tape measure home runs to go along with an impressive eye at the plate.

Soto's joined in the outfield this year by Adam Eaton in right and top prospect Victor Robles, whose speed rivals anyone in the game, manning center. Michael A. Taylor injured himself near the end of spring and until he's fully recovered, power hitter Matt Adams will see some time in the outfield as will veteran Howie Kendrick.

"It's exciting to know that you're on a team that wants to win and tries to put the best team on the field," Corbin says.

OPPOSITE: Members of the Washington Nationals stretch during spring training baseball practice in West Palm Beach, Fla.
JEFF ROBERSON / AP PHOTO

Anthony Rendon is the true star of this team to many, and even though he's entering the final year of his contract, it's a good bet that he'll be reupping on a long-term deal sometime soon. The third baseman hit .308 last year, with 24 homers and 92 knocks, and was exceptional as always at manning his position. Longtime Nats first baseman Ryan Zimmerman will try to rebound from another injury-plagued season, and hopefully provide more than the 85 games he played last year. He's only a year removed from a 36-homer season, though three of the past five seasons, he's seen action in less than 95 games.

Veteran Brian Dozier was signed to play the keystone and forms a new double-play combo with speedster Trea Turner, who led the league with 43 steals in 2018. In fact, speed is going to be a major weapon for the Nats this season.

Between Turner, Robles, Dozier and Eaton, this team can run, and manager Dave Martinez is not afraid to send his guys or call on the hit-and-run. The team brought in two longtime backstops this off-season to handle catching duties, with Yan Gomes coming over in a trade with Cleveland and Kurt Suzuki signing a two-year deal to return to the club after seven years.

Both offer solid framing skills and are above average with the bat for the catcher position.

The Nationals seem to have put together a team that is a perfect balance of pitching, offense and defense, and should be able to ride the strength of their arms all the way to the postseason.

"I think we're as good as any team in baseball from top to bottom," Corbin says. "Everyone's goal is to win a World Series. That's going to be ours. Our job now is to get better each and every day."

LEFT: Bullpen coach Henry Blanco, right, works with catcher Yan Gomes prior to an exhibition game.
BRYNN ANDERSON / AP PHOTO

LOWER LEFT: Pitcher Sean Doolittle throws a bullpen session at the Nationals complex.
JEFF ROBERSON / AP PHOTO

BELOW: Pitcher Max Scherzer runs sprints with teammates at the end of practice.
JEFF ROBERSON / AP PHOTO

OPPOSITE: Members of the Washington Nationals stretch at the start of a spring training practice.
JEFF ROBERSON / AP PHOTO

Members of the Washington Nationals and the New York Mets line the baselines during the national anthem prior to Opening Day March 28, 2019, in Washington.

NICK WASS / AP PHOTO

Turners Two Home Runs Help Nationals Get First Win

WASHINGTON — Still striving for their first win of the season, the Washington Nationals blew a three-run lead in the eighth inning and were locked in a tie game when Trea Turner came to the plate in the bottom of the ninth.

Nationals manager Dave Martinez seemingly knew what was coming, so he didn't bother to look.

Turner hit a drive into the left-field seats, his second home run of the game, to carry Washington past the New York Mets 6-5.

"Actually, I didn't even watch it," Martinez said. "I said, `I'm not going to watch, and when this ball goes over the wall we'll all celebrate.' And that's how it went down."

Turner earlier hit a three-run homer and also scored in the fifth to put Washington up 4-1. The Nationals let a 5-2 lead evaporate in the eighth before Turner ended it with a drive off Justin Wilson (1-1) that landed in the second row.

"It wasn't the way we scripted it, but we'll take it," Martinez said.

Left-hander Patrick Corbin gave up two runs, seven hits and two walks over six innings in his Washington debut.

"I just wanted to go out there and give us a chance to win after those first two games," Corbin said. "I'm not saying we had to win this, but I just wanted to go out there and do my best. Defense played great behind me. Yan [Gomes] called a great game."

After losing twice to New York, the Nationals avoided being swept in an opening series for the first time in a decade.

"I was thinking, we finally got our first win," Turner said. "We played pretty decent at times in the last three days, but to finally close one out was good."

Mets manager Mickey Callaway went through four pitchers before going to Wilson, who worked the eighth and got one out in the ninth before Turner connected on a 3-2 pitch.

"I knew there was a chance I would be in there late, with who had been used and stuff like that," Wilson said. "All I say is, good job by Trea and missed location by me."

During the postgame interview Turner deftly avoided the traditional Gatorade bath, which would have been downright chilling on a windy, raw day.

"It's way too cold," he said. "As you guys know, I'm a baby when it comes to cold."

Sean Doolittle (1-0) got the win despite allowing successive RBI singles in the New York eighth.

Corbin spent six seasons in Arizona before signing a $140 million, six-year deal with the Nationals, who hope he can fill out a rotation centered around stars Max Scherzer and Stephen Strasburg.

The starting rotation won't matter if the bullpen can't deliver. After giving up seven runs in two innings on Saturday, Washington relievers frittered away a three-run cushion in the eighth.

Tony Sipp allowed two hits, Trevor Rosenthal yielded a run-scoring single to Amed Rosario, and pinch-hitters Wilson Ramos and Juan Lagares hit two-out RBI singles off Doolittle to tie it.

That enabled Mets starter Zack Wheeler to avoid taking the loss. He gave up four runs in five innings.

"Knowing that we have an off-day tomorrow, and having dropped the first two games of the series, we were going all-in today," Doolittle said. "We were pushing our chips to the middle of the table."

Trea Turner, top right, dodges teammates Juan Soto (22) and Yan Gomes (10) attempt to douse him after he hit a walk-off home run to win the game in the ninth.

RIGHT: Nationals starting pitcher Patrick Corbin delivers a pitch.
NICK WASS / AP PHOTO

LOWER LEFT: Victor Robles reacts as he stands on second after hitting a double in the bottom of the sixth inning.
NICK WASS / AP PHOTO

LOWER RIGHT: Turner celebrates his three-run home run with Victor Robles, center, and Adam Eaton (2) during the third inning.
NICK WASS / AP PHOTO

OPPOSITE: Instead of the traditional Gatorade shower, Turner gets the bubblegum shower after hitting his winning homerun.
NICK WASS / AP PHOTO

The Soto Shuffle

It's an indelible image to Nats fans everywhere. Their prodigious young superstar Juan Soto stands in at the plate against a tough left-handed reliever in a big spot late in the game. He lays off a tough breaking ball low and away, his body leaning in toward the pitch. Then, while crouched over, he squares his body toward the pitcher, shuffling his feet while curling a small smile at the mound.

The "Soto Shuffle" is somehow both respectful and disrespectful, fun and serious, and lighthearted and cold-blooded.

"That started in the minor leagues," Soto explained when asked about his pitch-taking routine. "I like to get in the minds of the pitchers because sometimes they get scared. In the minor leagues some pitchers get scared, they say, 'oh, wow,' because [they've] never [seen] that before. I just try to get on their minds and all this stuff."

Of course, young minor league pitchers are a little more likely than MLB All-Stars to be scared off by a little dance from an opposing batter, but that hasn't stopped Soto from bringing the move to the big leagues. He has made an effort to pick his spots, though.

"I still do it here in the big leagues," he continued. "A couple of the guys tell me, 'hey, you can keep doing it, but do it in the right situation' and that's what I'm trying right now. Because in those tight moments everybody's paying attention, everybody wants to get the job done and if you get a little bit of confidence to get the job done, you get one step in front."

Surprisingly, neither Fangraphs nor Baseball-Reference offer statistics for "Juan Soto at-bats in which he shuffles at the pitcher," but anecdotally it sure feels like the young outfielder comes through in these big moments with regularity. He notably brought out the shuffle during his eventual game-winning at-bat in the eighth inning of this year's Wild Card Game.

"It fuels my confidence," Soto admitted. That confidence is clearly a crucial ingredient for any professional athlete, and Soto certainly isn't the first player to find ways to psyche himself up in important moments.

The reactions from opposing pitchers can be varied. For Soto, most see it for what it is: Soto hyping himself up, not attempting to show up the pitcher.

So, who had the funniest reaction to the little dance?

"It was last year," Soto answered when asked about the weirdest reaction he'd seen. "I did [it] against [current teammate Anibal] Sanchez and when I did it against him, he just started laughing on the mound. I mean, I start laughing too."

Soto appreciated how Sanchez, then a member of the rival Atlanta Braves, had fun with it. In fact, it may have helped his now teammate, if you ask Soto.

"He just started laughing and he couldn't stop, he just kept going," Soto continued while smiling. "He saw me and he just took that thing in the right way. And that was one of the pitchers that I never get a hit against, because he just stayed relaxed and he just enjoyed it. He likes when I do this, so I start, I just stopped doing it against him, but he keeps going and he just started laughing at it. And when he wasn't pitching he just saw me in the dugout and he just started doing it to me, and I'm like, that was the best reaction that I have received."

The "Soto Shuffle" is a small move coming from a big-name player and something that Nationals fans everywhere love seeing in huge moments. Hopefully, for them, we haven't seen the last of it in 2019.

LEFT: The sweet swing of Juan Soto.
MARK GOLDMAN / AP PHOTO

TOP: Soto gets a kiss from his father, Juan Jose Soto, right, after defeating the Milwaukee Brewers in the National League wild-card game.
ANDREW HARNIK / AP PHOTO

ABOVE: Soto shoots a smile to Nats fans.
BILL NICHOLS / AP PHOTO

Nationals Four Straight Home Runs Stun Padres

SAN DIEGO —With four swings in the span of seven pitches, the Washington Nationals put on a stunning power display that made major league history.

Howie Kendrick, Trea Turner, Adam Eaton and Anthony Rendon hit consecutive home runs off former Washington reliever Craig Stammen with one out in the eighth inning to lift Stephen Strasburg to another victory against his hometown San Diego Padres, 5-2.

The Nationals became the first team in major league history to accomplish the feat twice, according to the Elias Sports Bureau. The other time was July 27, 2017, against Milwaukee, when Brian Goodwin, Wilmer Difo, Bryce Harper and Ryan Zimmerman followed with long home runs.

Sunday's outburst surprised everyone.

"It's just one of those things. If you know how that happens, and how you can hit four in a row again, let me know, because we'll write a book and we'll be rich," Eaton said. "That play is contagious, when Howie did it, then Trea comes up and does the same thing, and then for me. If you could say four home runs, I would never be in that mix anywhere, the first one, the last one, the middle, anything to keep it going. I was happy I was in there. It's a pretty cool experience."

With the score tied at 1, Kendrick was pinch-hitting for Strasburg (7-3) when he started the homer parade with a shot to left, his 11th. Turner followed with a drive to center, his fourth, and Eaton's homer just cleared the wall in center, his sixth. Fans began booing then, and piled on after Rendon homered to right-center, his 12th.

Stammen (4-3) was the fourth of five Padres pitchers to throw on a "bullpen day." He pitched with Washington from 2009-2015 and signed with San Diego prior to the 2017 season.

Kendrick's homer went 421 feet, Turner's 425, Eaton's 402 and Rendon's 391.

"Nobody expected four home runs in a row but we'll take it," Kendrick said. "We take anything we can get as long as we get a W that's what's important."

Turner said it was exciting.

"I think we were pretty fired up when Howie hit his just because that gave us the lead and runs were hard to come by today. We were excited for that one but to do it three more times after that was pretty cool."

Said Rendon: "You don't want to be the one that doesn't hit the home run. It's just crazy. Glad we were on this side of it and not on the other side of it."

Manager Dave Martinez said he "liked the first one for sure, it put us ahead, then it was wow, wow, and wow. I was happy for Strasburg because he pitched an unbelievable game."

OPPOSITE: Howie Kendrick, right, is congratulated by third base coach Bob Henley after hitting the first of four straight home runs in the eighth inning.
ORLANDO RAMIREZ / AP PHOTO

Stammen said he thinks he became predictable and wondered if he was tipping pitches. He said there were a few pitches that he thought "weren't that bad that they smoked."

"It could be anything. There's many different reasons. That's never happened to me before," he said. "I wish I could explain. It's not fun to go through. I guess you can say it happens but I'm going to have to figure something out and get a little bit better."

Manager Andy Green said Stammen "always pitches on the edges. I'm assuming these aren't on the edges today."

Strasburg held San Diego to one run and six hits in seven innings while striking out six. He improved to 8-2 in his career against the Padres and to 4-1 in five starts at Petco Park. He pitched at West Hills High in suburban Santee before pitching for the late Hall of Famer Tony Gwynn at San Diego State.

Strasburg said the home run derby "was great to watch obviously, a lot of fun. You just try and keep the score as close as possible for the chance of that happening, and it did today."

Luis Perdomo started for the Padres, pitching 3 1/3 innings of two-hit ball and allowing only an unearned run.

Rendon also drove in a run on a groundout in the first.

OPPOSITE: Trea Turner with home run #2 during the eighth inning.
ORLANDO RAMIREZ / AP PHOTO

LEFT: Adam Eaton is congratulated by Anthony Rendon after hitting home run #3 during the eighth inning.
ORLANDO RAMIREZ / AP PHOTO

ABOVE: Rendon follows up with a home run of his own – the fourth straight of the inning - to solidify the win over the Padres.
ORLANDO RAMIREZ / AP PHOTO

Broken Nose Can't Slow Scherzer

WASHINGTON — With a broken nose, pronounced black eye and seven shutout innings, Max Scherzer provided a striking capper to the Washington Nationals' day-night doubleheader sweep of the Philadelphia Phillies.

Scherzer himself? He shrugged off his work in the Nationals' 2-0 victory as business as usual.

"Trust me, this thing looks a lot worse than it actually is," Scherzer said. "I felt zero pain. There's been plenty of other injuries where I felt a lot of pain and I've had to pitch through. I'll hang my hat on those starts, but tonight I felt zero pain. This is part of what you have to do. You take the ball every fifth time.

"That's my responsibility to the team, to make sure I always post, and I knew I could post tonight."

Brian Dozier and Victor Robles hit solo homers to support Scherzer (6-5) as Washington won for the 16th time in 23 games. Philadelphia has dropped seven of its past nine and 12 of 18.

Scherzer bunted a ball off his face during Tuesday's batting practice, but it didn't stop him from making his scheduled start. His injury might have provided an extra layer of intimidation in the form of a black eye more worthy of a boxing ring than a baseball diamond.

The three-time Cy Young Award winner sported a pronounced bruise arcing beneath his right eye, adding another hue to a glare that already featured one blue eye and one brown eye.

"Going out there and throwing, the only thing I had to deal with was the swelling underneath the eye," Scherzer said. "It was kind of jiggling around, and so in warm-ups I just had to get used to knowing what it was feeling like to throw the ball and just have that swelling."

While he wasn't at his most efficient on a humid night, piling up 117 pitches, Scherzer was rarely threatened. He struck out 10, yielded only four hits and permitted just two runners to reach scoring position. And he finished strong, striking out three in a row after Cesar Hernandez led off the seventh with a double.

"It really is one of the most impressive things I've seen in a while," Dozier said. "He's probably the best pitcher in our generation, and you don't get that status unless you take the ball every fifth day -- no matter if you're doing good, doing bad, you got a broken nose. You always want the ball."

Bryce Harper, Scherzer's former Nationals teammate, was 0-for-4 with four walks in the doubleheader and was loudly booed before each plate appearance -- especially in the better-attended nightcap. This series is his second trip back to Washington, where he played from 2012 to 2018, since signing a 13-year, $330 million contract with Philadelphia in March.

Dozier belted a two-out solo shot in the second off Jake Arrieta (6-6), who allowed two hits and struck out three over six innings and had the misfortune of matching up with Scherzer on the wrong day.

"Max is just one of the best to ever toe the rubber, honestly," Arietta said. "We have ran into him a couple of times. That's just what he does. He is tough to square up, and he is throwing three or four pitches for strikes with electric stuff. Just a tough one."

Wander Suero pitched a perfect eighth for Washington, and Sean Doolittle worked the ninth for his 15th save in 18 tries.

Sporting a black eye and broken nose
Max Scherzer throws his opening
pitch to the Philadelphia Phillies in the
second game of a doubleheader.
PATRICK SEMANSKY / AP PHOTO

OPPOSITE: Second baseman Brian Dozier hits a second inning solo home run.
MARK GOLDMAN / AP PHOTO

LEFT: Center fielder Victor Robles (16) celebrates with left fielder Juan Soto (22) after his eighth inning solo home run.
MARK GOLDMAN / AP PHOTO

BELOW: Starting pitcher Max Scherzer talks with catcher Kurt Suzuki in the dugout after shutting out the Phillies for seven innings.
MARK GOLDMAN / AP PHOTO

The Face of the Franchise

Ryan Zimmerman is deep into the autumn of his career, one that spans the entirety of the Washington Nationals' stay in D.C. The team's initial first round pick in 2005 was a September call-up during the tail-end of the Nats' inaugural season at RFK Stadium. He shined the following season as an everyday player, finishing second in the NL Rookie of the Year race. Zimmerman topped that off by hitting a walk-off home run in the first regular season game at Nationals Park the next March.

The problem was, there wasn't a lot of talent around Zimmerman at the time. It was an era of bad base running and dismal defense, misspelled uniforms and exploding sausage sandwiches in the skies. But the team was building for something special and Ryan Zimmerman was their cornerstone.

"He hasn't changed since I saw him at the University of Virginia. He's a pro's pro — and one of the great players that I've ever scouted," General Manager Mike Rizzo said. "A guy that's really given his all to the Washington Nationals. Physically, mentally and in the community he's been terrific. He's the face of the franchise for a reason."

The "face of the franchise" carries with it a ton of weight on the field and in the clubhouse. Production at the plate and making great plays in the field are tangible skills one can easily see; being the leader Zimmerman has been for the bulk of his career is not. But his teammates know and appreciate what Zim has done and continues to do on a daily basis.

"He's just an ultimate professional. A guy that goes out and puts his all into it — even banged up whatever it might be," Adam Eaton said. "Speaks highly of everybody. Somebody that you would follow into battle type of guy. There's a reason he's been the face of the organization for as long as he has been."

That means being the go-to quote in the clubhouse when it's not apparent who's had a big game; it also means being the guy who the young players look up to in the clubhouse as they try to navigate their way through the early stages of their careers. Zimmerman has been that kind of teammate which reliever Sean Doolittle knows from playing alongside him in college.

"When I was a freshman at Virginia and he was a junior, he was one of the top prospects in all of college baseball," Doolittle said. "And I got to watch the way he handled that pressure in the microscope and go about his business every day and was an awesome mentor to me."

Being "the guy" for so long means building friendships with teammates that may spend half a season or half a decade in D.C. And Zimmerman knows that while the 2019 Nationals are the team that finally won a playoff series, this World Series appearance also belongs to the Jayson Werths and Adam Laroches, former neighbors on his side of the clubhouse.

"It's definitely a culmination of a lot of guys that have been here," Zimmerman said. "We've had some chances and haven't come through, but they say you learn from your failures. All of those guys that were on those teams are part of this tonight even though they're not here."

After hitting .283 over 53 at bats in the season's final month, Zimmerman was no guarantee to be a fixture in the lineup. Autumn weather can defy explanation though; this October, Zimmerman has turned back the hands of the clock, hitting .290 with a homer and five RBI over nine games. His biggest hit was that broken-bat single in the Wild Card Game that set up Juan Soto's go-ahead single in the eighth inning.

"What he's doing now does not surprise me one bit," Manager Davey Martinez said. "The biggest thing for him was his health. If you get a healthy Ryan Zimmerman, the product on the field speaks for itself."

Zimmerman was the first-round pick of the Nationals in the 2005 MLB Draft. He has gone on to hit 270 home runs in his 15-year career.

NICK WASS / MARK GOLDMAN / MATT SLOCUM / AP PHOTO

Turner Hits for Second Career Cycle

WASHINGTON — A smile crept across Trea Turner's face as he pulled into second base in the seventh inning of Tuesday night's 11-1 win. A rowdy crowd of 22,612 fans at Nationals Park showered him with a standing ovation while the home dugout stood and cheered.

This was all a familiar feeling for Turner, who had just hit for the cycle for the second time in his career (once again against the Rockies), making him just the 26th player in MLB history to accomplish the feat more than once and the third player to do so against the same team. But in that moment -- the middle of an eight-run seventh inning that catapulted the Nationals to victory over the Rockies -- what Turner felt most was relief.

"I didn't screw it up this time," he said with a smile.

Turner was referring to a game against the White Sox last month in Chicago, when he finished a single shy of the cycle, unable to get the final hit he needed in his final two at-bats. He missed his first chance Tuesday night when he grounded into an inning-ending double play in the sixth inning, spoiling his opportunity at the cycle at a point when he was not guaranteed another at-bat.

When he got to the plate again in the seventh, however, Turner capitalized. He lined a 1-0 pitch from Rockies reliever Jairo Díaz into the gap in right-center field and glided into second base with a place in history secure (again). He finished the night 4-for-5 with two RBIs and a pair of runs scored.

"For me, it's almost [funnier] than anything that I got lucky enough to get all the right hits," Turner said. "I think it's kind of a lucky stat, just because you've got to put the ball in the right place at the right time. And I ended up doing that."

Yes, some luck is required, but Turner's combination of speed and power at the plate always makes him a threat to complete one of baseball's most special feats for a hitter. This was the fourth cycle in Nationals history, with Turner's pair joining Brad Wilkerson and Cristian Guzman.

"It's a feat that doesn't happen often," Nationals manager Dave Martinez said. "To be able to do it twice. That, to me, is a testament to how good a player Trea really is."

Colorado has also contributed to a plethora of cycles throughout team history. Turner hit the 10th cycle against the Rockies, with the previous nine all coming at Coors Field. In fact, the previous 18 cycles the Rockies have been involved in since becoming a team in 1993 had all come at Coors Field, which opened in '95.

That includes Turner's first cycle from April 25, 2017, which he finished with a triple, sliding into third base wearing a fleece mask and long sleeves on a cold night in Colorado.

"It was terrible in Colorado, I was pretty miserable," Turner said. "And I was coming back from I think a hamstring pull. I remember when I hit the triple, [first-base coach at the time] Davey Lopes was yelling at me to go easy. And I was like: 'Screw it, this is probably my one and only shot.' So I went for it."

He went for it again on Tuesday night, although the weather conditions at Nationals Park were much better.

Turner began the game by launching a leadoff homer, the ninth of his career, which matches Alfonso Soriano for the most in Nationals history (2005-present). He collected a two-out single in the second and knocked a triple into the right-field corner in the fifth -- the first three legs of the cycle all off Colorado starter Peter Lambert.

Then he finished it off in the seventh, putting him in a select group in baseball history. Turner joins Fred Clarke (in 1901 and '03, against the Reds) and Christian Yelich (last season, also against the Reds) as the other players in MLB history to record two cycles against the same team. Adrián

Trea Turner watches his first inning
solo home run leave the park.
PATRICK SEMANSKY / AP PHOTO

Beltré owns the Major League record with three, a fact Turner said he had heard recently, although he wasn't sure he would be challenging that mark anytime soon.

"It's a hard game, and to get four hits in one game is hard to do," Turner said. "To have four different ones is, I think, a little bit of luck. But also, at the same time, a little humbling to be with those guys."

OPPOSITE: Trea Turner, left, rounds the bases past Colorado Rockies first baseman Daniel Murphy after hitting a solo home run.
PATRICK SEMANSKY / AP PHOTO

ABOVE: Starting pitcher Stephen Strasburg picked up his 13th win of the year against the Rockies.
PATRICK SEMANSKY / AP PHOTO

LEFT: Victor Robles, left, slides safely past Rockies catcher Chris Iannetta to score on a throwing error by left fielder Ian Desmond in the seventh inning.
PATRICK SEMANSKY / AP PHOTO

31

King of the Hill

Stephen Strasburg is used to the process by now. After dominating opposing hitters for more than 100 pitches, Washington Nationals teammates Gerardo Parra and Anibal Sanchez, and sometimes others, surround him, wrap him in a hug, rock back and forth, and savor the moment.

It is partly a bit — Strasburg's public face ranges from wooden to laconic to occasional bursts of engaged reticence, and so the Nationals' provocateurs are determined to wring joy out of their 6-foot-5, 230-pound anchor.

"You just gotta embrace it," Strasburg says, apparently without a hint of irony. "They start squeezing me a little bit harder every time. But that's OK."

It's no surprise, then, that Wednesday night's embrace — future Hall of Famer Max Scherzer even joined the fun this time — was a little tighter. There is a chance Strasburg has thrown his last pitch this season, thanks in large part to his handiwork against the Houston Astros in Game 2 of the World Series.

The win gave the Nationals a 2-0 World Series lead, and a shot to win their first championship in franchise history by merely winning two of the next three games at home.

And should that come to pass, let history reflect that this October, for all the Nationals' big hits and relentless baserunning and shark tales, belongs to Strasburg.

He has pitched in five games and the Nationals have won them all, posting a 1.93 ERA and striking out 40 batters in 30 innings.

"He's become a premier pitcher," says manager Dave Martinez, "a big-game pitcher."

Like the win in Game 2 of the NL Division Series to get them back in the series against the 106-win Los Angeles Dodgers. Surviving the early fusillade in Game 5 of that NLDS so the Nationals could eventually prevail in 10 innings.

Squeezing the last hope out of the St. Louis Cardinals, striking out 12 of them over seven innings with no earned runs in Game 3 of the NLCS.

And then, against the highly disciplined and best-in-the-majors Astros lineup, shrugging off a first-inning Alex Bregman home run to post five gutty zeroes and keep the game's leverage level.

Lest we forget, this run began with three shutout relief innings against the Milwaukee Brewers in the wild-card game, a night Scherzer stumbled, Strasburg picked him up and held the line when the Nationals fell in a 3-1 hole.

"You can't say enough about how good he's been," says reliever Sean Doolittle. "I thought that was one of his most impressive outings — that three innings in the wild card game. He just kept going after that."

All the way into Wednesday night, 2-2 game, sixth inning and Minute Maid Park ready to will the Astros into tying this series after Yuli Gurriel's one-out double.

Strasburg fell behind Yordan Alvarez 2-0 before Martinez opted for a debatable intentional walk. Strasburg then battled Carlos Correa, Suzuki and he jogging their brains to change up the sequences from previous plate appearances. Faced with a full count, a delirious crowd and a seasoned playoff hitter, Strasburg deployed a full-count changeup. Correa popped out to second base.

Pinch hitter Kyle Tucker offered similar resistance, stretching Strasburg to eight pitches. Strasburg had a little something for him - a 3-2 curveball

that he waved meekly at.

It was ruled a called strike three. More accurately, it was a burgeoning playoff beast schooling a rookie.

"Any pitch," says Nats catch Kurt Suzuki, "any time. He's got so many weapons to get you out with. You never really know what pitch is coming. If he changes up his patterns and we do a good job of sequencing it becomes tough for the hitters."

Sequencing and execution and all that are great, but October is as much about owning the moment as harnessing your stuff.

"To me, what's so impressive is how he's able to control his off-speed pitches and pitch with finesse in moments when there's tons of energy in the ballpark," says Doolittle. "It's almost like he's able to lower his heart rate to a point where he's calmer than the hitter. He's not getting caught up in the moment."

Strasburg said his first World Series start did not kick his adrenaline up any higher than his previous playoff starts.

But it did remind him why he's out here.

"As a kid, you have those dreams," he says. "You play the game because you love it. And I love playing this game, and I'm going to play it as long as I can.

"Hopefully, there's championships, but you have to focus on what you can control. I'm just enjoying every minute and soak it all in."

LEFT: Strasburg pauses before delivering a pitch against the Phillies.
MATT SLOCUM / AP PHOTO

TOP: Strasburg throws a pitch during Game 5 of the National League Division Series.
MARCIO JOSE SANCHEZ / AP PHOTO

ABOVE: Strasburg takes a break between innings to work on his bubble blowing skills.
MARK GOLDMAN / AP PHOTO

Nats Stun Mets in Wild Walk-Off Win

WASHINGTON — The ball had barely been launched into the air, but Kurt Suzuki knew it right off the bat. He immediately turned and pointed toward his dugout, where his teammates had already begun jumping up and down, spilling out onto the field and erupting with joy.

When Suzuki's walk-off, three-run homer off Edwin Diaz landed in the left-field seats, it completed the largest ninth-inning comeback win in franchise history, an improbable victory after the Nationals trailed by six runs entering the frame. Washington rattled off seven hits and seven runs in the final frame to pull off a stunning 11-10 victory over New York, storming all the way back to seal one of the wildest finishes in club history.

"Boom," manager Dave Martinez said to begin his postgame press conference as a group of fans sitting in the club seats behind home plate cheered. "What do you want me to say? Boom."

Or take it from first baseman Ryan Zimmerman, who has played in more games than any player in Nats history: "The craziest. I don't know if it's a record or not, but it's got to be pretty close. It's been a crazy year. That's the only way to kind of sum it up, for me, for the team, for everybody."

These Nationals are starting to make a habit out of overcoming adversity, whether it's rebounding from a slow start to the season or erasing countless bullpen meltdowns. And yet, nothing compared to what they pulled off this night.

They won this game after giving up five runs during a disastrous top of the ninth, which included a mental lapse from shortstop Trea Turner, who failed to turn an easy double play because he forgot there was only one out. Even Max Scherzer, who started the game and gave up four runs in six innings, admitted he had stopped watching the ninth inning from the video room after his start. And who could blame him? Teams leading by six runs or more entering the bottom of the ninth had been 274-0 this season.

"Let's be honest, I don't think we thought it was going to happen either," Zimmerman said. "A lot of us have been around baseball for a long time. Once it starts going, the pressure shifts obviously squarely on their shoulders. Stuff like that is not supposed to happen. It's a crazy sport. Crazy things happen."

But in the dugout at the start of the ninth inning, Martinez never panicked. In fact, he was so calm before the inning began that second baseman Asdrúbal Cabrera wondered what was up. Stay positive, the sometimes overly-optimistic Martinez reminded him. And then the hits began.

"I think that's when I started believing we can come back," Cabrera said.

Victor Robles started the inning with a single against Paul Sewald. After Howie Kendrick flied out to right field, Turner began to atone for his mistake with a

OPPOSITE: Kurt Suzuki (28) celebrates after hitting the game winning, walk-off three-run home run against the New York Mets.

run-scoring double. Cabrera and Anthony Rendon collected back-to-back singles, which knocked Sewald out of the game. He was replaced by lefty Luis Avilan, who didn't fare much better. Juan Soto singled through the right side of the infield, ending Avilan's night and loading the bases. Then came Diaz, who surrendered a two-run double to Zimmerman, which set up Suzuki for one of the biggest hits of this Nationals season.

"With the at-bats everybody was putting on in that inning, I didn't want to be the guy to kill the rally," Suzuki said. "I wanted to come through just like everybody else. I think hitting is contagious, and when you see these guys putting up quality at-bats when you're down by six runs, it makes you want to go up there and keep the line moving."

"When I came in here, I didn't really know what just happened," Mets center fielder Brandon Nimmo said. "It kind of just seemed like a bad dream. To come back from seven runs down in the bottom of the ninth against guys throwing 99 miles an hour, I don't really have words for that."

Suzuki ripped his helmet off and threw his hands up into the sky as he rounded third and headed toward his teammates, who were waiting to dogpile him at home plate. It was his third career walk-off home run and his first since 2008. After he emerged from the mob, one of the first people he found was Turner, and they shared a huge embrace behind the plate.

"I've been in that spot, and you feel like you're on an island by yourself," Suzuki said. "It's horrible. Trea's one of the best players in the game. Things like that happen, and that's what teammates are for, to pick each other up and move forward."

ABOVE: Kurt Suzuki, right, is doused by Trea Turner.
PATRICK SEMANSKY / AP PHOTO

OPPOSITE: Nationals players greet Suzuki (28) as he approaches home plate after hitting the game winning home run.
PATRICK SEMANSKY / AP PHOTO

Nats Clinch Wild Card

WASHINGTON — Dave Martinez's words were drenched with emotion as he stood in a booze-soaked clubhouse, Washington Nationals players celebrating all around after clinching an NL wild card exactly four months after they woke up with a 19-31 record and calls for him to be replaced as manager.

Quite a turnaround for Martinez -- and for his club.

"They don't want to go home. They want to keep playing," Martinez said, wearing the same red T-shirt reading "Let's get wild" as his players had on. "They don't quit."

Trea Turner's go-ahead grand slam in the sixth inning lifted Washington to a 6-5 comeback victory over the Philadelphia Phillies for a doubleheader sweep that assured the Nationals of extending their season and eliminated the Phillies from playoff contention.

"They're resilient. Tonight they were down, but they never feel like they're out," Martinez said. "They stick together. And here we are, going to the postseason."

He missed three full games and part of another this month because of a heart issue; the 54-year-old skipper was back in the dugout four days after having a cardiac catheterization.

"They keep telling me how much they want to play for me," Martinez said in the mayhem, his voice cracking. "And I tell them it's not about me. It's about us. Just play for us."

Washington is returning to the playoffs for the fifth time in eight years after sitting out October in 2018, when the team went 82-80 in Martinez's rookie year as a manager.

Things started roughly in 2019: Washington was 12 games below .500 after a loss on May 23 concluded a four-game sweep at the New York Mets.

At that point, the Nationals were fourth in the NL East, thanks to defensive sloppiness, bad baserunning and, above all, unreliable-as-can-be work from the bullpen.

But Martinez retained his always-sunny disposition and remained in his post, unwilling to publicly criticize his players and, in a participation-trophy sort of way, often pointing out how hard they had tried in defeat.

Eventually, things clicked. Washington went on a real roll, even playing winning baseball while Max Scherzer took two trips to the injured list with a back muscle problem.

Perhaps fittingly, it was three-time Cy Young Award winner Scherzer (11-7) who got the clinching win despite a rocky start, allowing a pair of

homers to Brad Miller as Washington fell behind 4-2. But much like the way the entire season went, the Nationals dug themselves out.

"We knew nothing was going to be won or lost in the first five months," said Turner, who had three hits in the day's first game, a 4-1 win for the Nationals, "and now we're in a good spot."

The Nationals entered Tuesday hoping to beat Philadelphia twice plus get a loss by the Chicago Cubs at Pittsburgh -- and each of those things happened.

Right after center fielder Victor Robles made a running catch for the last out of the second game in Washington, the Nationals Park scoreboard showed the Cubs vs. the Pirates.

Many of Washington's players stood on their stadium's infield and watched the end of the Cubs' 9-2 defeat, then started celebrating there before heading indoors for the real deal, which included red cans of Budweiser, blue cans of Bud Light, white cans of Stella Artois and bottles of Campo Viejo Cava.

"With everything we went through as a group," reliever Sean Doolittle said, "it feels so much sweeter."

Anthony Rendon delivered two sacrifice flies to raise his majors-leading

Third base coach Bob Henley greets Trea Turner as he rounds third after hitting a grand slam in the sixth inning.
PATRICK SEMANSKY / AP PHOTO

RBI total to 124 in the opening victory, a result that also eliminated Philadelphia and $330 million outfielder Bryce Harper, the ex-Nationals star.

"I've got no hard feelings towards them at all. They're a great team. They're a great organization," Harper said. "That's why they're at where they're at right now."

In the nightcap, Washington trailed 4-2 entering the sixth -- and at that moment, about 250 miles away, the Cubs were leading the Pirates 1-0.

Everything changed within minutes.

While Washington was loading the bases against Aaron Nola (12-7) with two walks and a single -- setting the stage for Turner's 18th homer of the season and second career slam, which came off Jared Hughes -- the Cubs were imploding during the Pirates' seven-run seventh.

Turner's drive to left made it 6-4, and he celebrated with the Nationals' customary dugout dance line and a curtain call. The clubhouse party included a loud rendition, naturally, of "Baby Shark," the walkup song for midseason acquisition Gerardo Parra, who brought a dose of levity to his new club.

LEFT: Center fielder Victor Robles (16) is all smiles after the Nats clinched the wild card berth.
PATRICK SEMANSKY / AP PHOTO

LOWER LEFT: Max Scherzer, left, and Gerardo Parra celebrate with a selfie.
PATRICK SEMANSKY / AP PHOTO

LOWER RIGHT: Manager Dave Martinez, right, gets doused as he celebrates in the clubhouse.
PATRICK SEMANSKY / AP PHOTO

OPPOSITE: Trea Turner, second from right, celebrates with teammates Howie Kendrick, from left, Victor Robles and Asdrubal Cabrera after hitting his grand slam.
PATRICK SEMANSKY / AP PHOTO

Soto Lifts Nats to 4-3 Comeback Wild-Card Win

WASHINGTON — After all the heartache and close calls, all the early exits, maybe it makes sense that a 20-year-old kid who never had been to the postseason, Juan Soto, would help the Washington Nationals finally advance.

Soto delivered a bases-loaded single against Milwaukee closer Josh Hader that scored three runs with two outs in the eighth inning, thanks in part to an error by rookie outfielder Trent Grisham, and the Nationals came back to beat the Brewers 4-3 in the NL wild-card game.

"We started off horrible, as we all know, and we vowed that we wouldn't quit," Nationals manager Dave Martinez said, talking about the year as a whole but sounding like he could have meant this particular evening. "I told the boys, 'I promise you, stay with it, don't quit, this will turn around.' And it did. And here we are today."

The Nationals carry a nine-game winning streak into their best-of-five NL Division Series against the league-best Dodgers.

Game 1 is Thursday in Los Angeles, and some in the sellout crowd of 42,993 chanted "Beat LA! Beat LA!" as members of the Nationals began their celebration on the infield with family members.

That included Soto's father leaping onto his back and tackling him amid the excitement.

The Nationals, who moved to Washington from Montreal before the 2005 season, had been 0-3 in winner-take-all postseason games -- all NLDS Game 5 losses at home, by a grand total of four runs. Indeed, eight of their past nine playoff losses had been by one run apiece.

This time, it went the other way.

"We've been here a bunch of times. Never kind of broke through," said Ryan Zimmerman, the Nationals' first draft pick back in 2005, so someone who has been through all the disappointment. "Finally caught a break tonight."

It was Zimmerman's broken-bat bloop single as a pinch hitter that helped load the bases in the eighth off Hader, who took the loss.

Hader hit another pinch hitter, Michael A. Taylor, a ruling that stood up when the Brewers challenged, according to Major League Baseball, because there wasn't "clear and convincing evidence to overturn the call."

Said Hader: "Definitely looked like it got the bat, but it also got his hand."

Hader, who had 37 saves this season, also walked Anthony Rendon, filling the bags and bringing Soto to the plate.

What was Soto thinking right then?

"Just get a base hit up the middle," he said, "and try to help to tie the game."

The runner-up for 2018 NL Rookie of the Year did more than that. Soto ripped

OPPOSITE: Juan Soto drives in three runs with a single in the bottom of the eighth inning to put the Nationals up 4-3 over the Milwaukee Brewers.

ANDREW HARNIK / AP PHOTO

ABOVE: Stephen Strasburg struck out four in his three innings of impressive relief work.
PATRICK SEMANSKY / AP PHOTO

TOP RIGHT: Trea Turner, right, shakes hands with third base coach Bob Henley after hitting a solo home run in the third inning.
PATRICK SEMANSKY / AP PHOTO

RIGHT: Ryan Zimmerman hits a broken bat single in the eighth inning.
MARK GOLDMAN / AP PHOTO

OPPOSITE: The Washington Nationals celebrate in the clubhouse.
MARK GOLDMAN / AP PHOTO

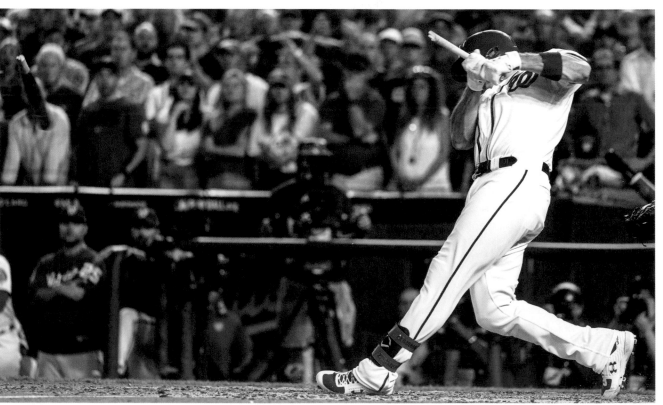

a 96-mph fastball to right, and the ball skipped under Grisham's glove for an error. That allowed the go-ahead run to cross the plate and Soto to get to second, then turn for third.

"Right guy, right spot," winning pitcher Stephen Strasburg said about Soto.

Eventually, Soto was caught in a rundown to end the inning, but that didn't matter: He had turned a 3-1 deficit into a lead, and so he clapped his hands, then pounded his chest and high-fived third base coach Bob Henley, before shouting "Let's go!" and its Spanish equivalent, "Vamonos!"

"The inning was an ugly inning," Brewers manager Craig Counsell said. "Crazy things happen."

After Max Scherzer fell behind 3-0 by giving up homers to Yasmani Grandal in the first and Eric Thames in the second, Strasburg replaced him in the sixth and threw three scoreless innings to earn the win in the first relief appearance of his major league career, regular season or playoffs.

Daniel Hudson pitched the ninth for the save, getting Ben Gamel to fly out to the warning track in center with a man on to end it.

"Hats off for us to for continuing to fight, because we know if we could

keep it close we could have a chance at the end," said Trea Turner, who got Washington within 3-1 with a solo shot off Brandon Woodruff in the third.

It wasn't until the eighth, though, that the Nationals would push more runs across. Just the sort of dramatic turnaround they pulled off this season, going from 19-31 in May to playoff team.

And now it continues.

"Kind of sums up our season, the way this game went," Zimmerman said. "We'll take it and we'll move on."

Mad Max

When the Washington Nationals signed Max Scherzer in January of 2015, there was question by many in the baseball world why a team with so much starting pitching already would hand out a huge contract to another starter. After the offseason concluded baseball executives in an anonymous poll voted Scherzer's deal the "worst deal" of that offseason.

As we sit here four years later in 2019, that narrative could not be further from the truth. You could make a solid argument the Scherzer' deal is the best free agent signing in baseball history, and after striking out 10 in seven shutout innings with a black eye and broken nose, the legend of Mad Max continued to grow.

Since coming to Washington in 2015, Scherzer has recorded double-digit strikeouts in a game 63 times, has never had an earned run average above 2.96, and has started at least 31 games in his four full seasons.

The future Hall-of-Famer also has been named an All-Star in each of his first four seasons in D.C. and has won two Cy-Young awards, and could potentially add another this season.

It is easy to focus on the stats and be in awe about just how dominant Mad Max has been, but equally impressive is his presence on and off the mound. After breaking his nose in batting practice on a Tuesday earlier in the year, everyone in the world questioned if he would be able to take the mound for his scheduled start on Wednesday, except Max himself.

Scherzer knew his team needed him in the vital series against the division-rival Philadelphia Phillies, and nothing was going to stop him from taking that mound. Broken-nose, black eye and all, Scherzer came out and absolutely dominated the Phillies.

"(He) is one of the best pitchers in the league. Day in and day out, start in and start out, he gives you an opportunity to win," Nats GM Mike Rizzo said of Scherzer. "He gives you his best. He leaves everything on the mound each and every time. The days that he's got four or five pitches going and he's throwing strikes, those are the dominant days and those are the things that's must-see TV."

Rizzo hasn't been shy about framing Scherzer discussions in the proper historical context, and to remind Nats fans exactly what they're seeing.

"I think that we're seeing something from a Major League pitcher that we're very fortunate, because we get to see this every fifth day," Rizzo said. "This is historical stuff. This is one of the great pitchers of our time and a Hall of Fame caliber guy. A guy who just, he leaves it on the mound each and every day.

"When he's great, he's great. When he's just good, it's fun to watch because he just leaves everything on the mound. I think those are the times that really separate him from the great pitchers, is when he's struggling for command or he's struggling to get guys out, you just see the competitiveness come out of him. Those are the games I love to see."

Asked whether it was Scherzer's talent, or his moxie, that first drew his attention, Rizzo acknowledged that Scherzer's mental makeup is what's driven him into historical company.

"It's just the attitude," he said. "That's the reason we took him in 2006, was the way he went after people. It was his competitiveness on the mound. You know, his stuff was good. It wasn't elite. He came into the league and was a good pitcher, and was traded and that type of thing. This guy's makeup made him what he is.

"He has some God-given ability, but this guy squeezes out every ounce of ability and capability that he has in each and every start."

"Like I said, when he's going good, it's fun to watch," Rizzo added. "Those are the 15-strikeout days. Also, when he's just going okay is really when you see the competitiveness and what makes Max Scherzer different than most every other pitcher in the game, is that he wills himself to win and he wills himself to go the extra inning, the extra pitch."

"He talks about it all the time, the last 15," he said. "Those last 15 pitches when he's emptying the tank is probably, for me, one of the most enjoyable, compelling, competitive things to watch in all of sports."

LEFT: Scherzer has won 79 games in his five years with the Nationals.
DAVID JOHN GRIFFIN / AP PHOTO

TOP: Scherzer pumps his fist after getting another strike out.
ALEX BRANDON / AP PHOTO

ABOVE: Scherzer, left, shakes hands with Washington Capitals left wing Alex Ovechkin.
MARK GOLDMAN / AP PHOTO

Members of the Washington Nationals warm up before Game 1
of the National League Divisional Series.
MARK J. TERRILL / AP PHOTO

Dodgers Cruise Past Nats in NLDS Opener

LOS ANGELES — The Dodgers overpowered the Nationals on the mound and at the plate, extending the dominance that led to a franchise-record 106 victories in the regular season right on into the playoffs.

Walker Buehler allowed one hit over six innings, Max Muncy drove in three runs and Los Angeles capitalized on mistakes to beat Washington 6-0 in Game 1 of their NL Division Series.

"Oh, they're good. They're really good," Nationals manager Dave Martinez said. "That's why they have been in the postseason so many years in a row."

Buehler struck out eight, walked three and retired his final seven batters after earning the start over veterans Clayton Kershaw and Hyun-Jin Ryu, whose 2.32 ERA was lowest in the majors this season.

"Walker, time and time again, just knows how to temper, control his emotions and transfer that into the delivery, the execution of pitches," Dodgers manager Dave Roberts said.

Dodgers rookie Gavin Lux and Joc Pederson slugged pinch-hit solo homers in the eighth.

Nationals first baseman Howie Kendrick had two grounders roll under his glove, the second leading to the Dodgers' second run in the fifth.

Washington's Patrick Corbin stumbled through a rocky first inning. He issued four walks, joining Art Reinhart of the St. Louis Cardinals as the only pitchers to walk that many in the first inning they ever pitched in the postseason.

"That first inning was the game," Roberts said. "That really set the tone."

Corbin walked three in a row with two outs in the 31-pitch inning. Yan Gomes was charged with a passed ball, too, and Muncy drew a free pass with the bases loaded to put the Dodgers in front.

"Walked a lot of guys, chased a lot of bad pitches," Martinez said. "When you're walking guys and not hitting, it's tough to win ballgames."

Corbin gave up two runs -- one earned -- and three hits in six innings. The left-hander struck out nine and finished with five walks.

"It just didn't seem like he had his command," Muncy said. "We did a really good job of not chasing balls out of the zone."

Cody Bellinger walked with two outs and scored on an error by Kendrick in the fifth that made it 2-0. Third baseman Anthony Rendon made a diving stop on Chris Taylor's single down the line, but his throw to first wasn't in time and Bellinger went to third.

Muncy's grounder rolled through Kendrick's legs for an error, scoring Bellinger, and Taylor got thrown out at the plate to end the inning.

OPPOSITE: Anthony Rendon makes a diving attempt at a ball hit by the Dodgers Chris Taylor during the fifth inning.
MARK J. TERRILL / AP PHOTO

"I wouldn't change anything about the way I tried to make that play. Just one of those times you just miss it," Kendrick said.

In the fourth, Muncy singled leading off. Corey Seager followed with a hit that got past a diving Kendrick at first and rolled into right, sending Muncy to third. But then Corbin settled down and retired the next three batters to end the inning.

"Mechanically, was rushing a little bit. Was cutting my fastball," Corbin said. "Later on was able to get back to my sinker and everything else felt good after that."

Muncy added a two-run single with two outs in the seventh, extending the lead to 4-0.

The Nationals loaded the bases in the fourth on three walks by Buehler. He escaped when Asdrubal Cabrera tapped the ball back to the mound and Buehler flipped to first to end the inning.

"From that first throw, he was on point," Roberts said. "That's a really good lineup over there and for him to go six, we needed that."

Juan Soto, who had the key hit in the wild-card win over Milwaukee, singled in the second and Trea Turner doubled in the ninth off Joe Kelly for the Nationals' only hits.

LEFT: Fernando Rodney reacts after the Dodgers Max Muncy's two-run single during the seventh inning.
MARK J. TERRILL / AP PHOTO

ABOVE: Patrick Corbin is not pleased after walking in a run in the first inning.
MARK J. TERRILL / AP PHOTO

OPPOSITE: Juan Soto slams his bat in frustration after striking out.
MARK J. TERRILL / AP PHOTO

Nationals Pitching Dominates Dodgers in Game 2

LOS ANGELES — The bullpen gate swung open and out trotted ... Max Scherzer? Yep, Washington's ace surprised the Los Angeles Dodgers and even a few teammates in the eighth inning Friday night.

"All the chips are on the table right now," Scherzer said.

"We weren't expecting that," Dodgers manager Dave Roberts said.

Stephen Strasburg turned in another dominant playoff outing, Scherzer struck out the side and Washington held off the Dodgers 4-2 to even their National League Division Series at a game apiece.

Pitching on the shortest rest of his career, Strasburg took a perfect game into the fifth inning while outdueling Clayton Kershaw. Strasburg pitched one-run ball for six innings and struck out 10, lowering his career postseason ERA to 0.64 -- the best in history for players with at least four starts. He edged out Dodgers great Sandy Koufax (0.95 ERA), who watched Game 2 from the front row.

"There's obviously a lot of expectations, there's a lot of excitement in games," Strasburg said, "but I really tried over the years to train my mind into thinking that every single game is just as important and just sticking to my approach."

Rookie Will Smith broke up Strasburg's perfect bid with a two-out single. The three-time All-Star gave up his first earned run in 23 consecutive postseason innings dating to the 2014 NLDS against San Francisco and limited Los Angeles to three hits and no walks.

"Stras was on top of his game and really throwing the daylights out of the ball," Scherzer said.

Scherzer came on for the eighth and struck out Gavin Lux, Chris Taylor and Joc Pederson on 14 pitches. The 35-year-old right-hander threw 77 pitches in the NL wild-card game Tuesday, yet he topped out at 99 mph in his fourth career playoff relief appearance.

"I felt I could really go one inning and recover from that," Scherzer said. "I said whatever the situation is, I'm ready to pitch."

Justin Turner led off the ninth with a ground-rule double off Hudson, spurring hope from a chanting, clapping sellout crowd of 53,086. A.J. Pollock struck out, and then Cody Bellinger popped up to shallow left. Third baseman Anthony Rendon misjudged the ball but recovered and made the catch while he tumbled over. The goateed All-Star smiled wide as he stood.

"The ball kept going and I kept thinking, 'Where the hell is our left fielder at?'" Rendon said. "He didn't call it so I knew I had to catch it."

Martinez then intentionally walked Max Muncy, who had hit a solo shot off

OPPOSITE: Anthony Rendon makes an incredible diving catch on a short fly ball hit by the Dodgers Cody Bellinger during the ninth inning.
MARK J. TERRILL / AP PHOTO

ABOVE: Adam Eaton, left, scores safely past Dodgers catcher Will Smith on a double by Anthony Rendon.
MARK J. TERRLL / AP PHOTO

RIGHT: Howie Kendrick delivers a RBI single.
MARCIO JOSE SANCHEZ / AP PHOTO

OPPOSITE: Daniel Hudson celebrates after striking out the Dodgers Corey Seager to end Game 2.
MARK J. TERRILL / AP PHOTO

Sean Doolittle in the seventh, before Daniel Hudson walked Smith to load the bases. Corey Seager fouled off four fastballs before Hudson got him to swing over a slider.

"It was a little more entertaining than I wanted it to be," Hudson said. "I didn't have the greatest command."

The Nationals took a 4-2 lead in the top of the eighth on Asdrubal Cabrera's pinch-hit RBI single.

Los Angeles finally scored in the sixth on Turner's sacrifice fly after Matt Beaty's pinch-hit single and Pederson's double. With the tying run at the plate,

Pollock lined out to Strasburg to end the inning.

Until Smith broke through, the Dodgers' closest attempt at a hit came in the third when Kershaw's sinking line drive was grabbed by diving left fielder Juan Soto. The Dodgers struck out 17 times against Nationals pitching.

Kershaw ran into immediate trouble, with Trea Turner doubling on his first pitch of the game. After Adam Eaton popped out to third, Kershaw walked Rendon and hit Soto to load the bases. Howie Kendrick, who had two errors in a Game 1 defeat, followed with a run-scoring single.

The Nationals tacked on a pair of two-out runs in the second for a 3-0 lead. Kershaw hit Victor Robles leading off, and Robles moved to second on a sacrifice bunt by Strasburg. Eaton singled in Robles, and Rendon followed with a double off the wall in center.

"The second inning was not good. That was what decided the game really," Kershaw said.

Big Sixth Inning Lifts LA Past Nats

WASHINGTON — The Washington Nationals' postseason strategy of milking as many outs as possible out of their front-of-the-line starters hit a snag in Game 3 in the National League Division Series. The snag being that when the Los Angeles Dodgers' bats wake up, it may not matter who is pitching.

The Dodgers pounded the Nats for seven runs in the sixth inning, changing the tempo of both this game and perhaps the series, as L.A. earned a 10-4 win and took a 2-1 series advantage.

The Dodgers can advance to the NL Championship Series for the fourth consecutive year by closing the best-of-five NLDS in Game 4 at Washington, when LA sends Rich Hill to the mound against Max Scherzer.

Everything seemed to be going well enough for the Nats heading into the sixth inning. Anibal Sanchez, who manager Davey Martinez opted to start instead of ace Scherzer, was brilliant through five innings. He struck out nine, allowing just a Max Muncy homer.

In came starter-turned-reliever Patrick Corbin, the lefty who started -- and lost -- the opener and hadn't made a relief appearance since 2017, when he only made one.

After Dodgers MVP candidate Cody Bellinger snapped his 0-for-8 start to the series with a single -- he would add a double later in the inning -- Corbin struck out the next two hitters. That's when it all fell apart for Washington.

David Freese, the MVP of the 2011 NLCS and World Series for St. Louis, singled to put runners on the corners.

"He has to be going down as one of the greatest October players of all time," Muncy said of Freese. "I don't care what anyone says. He has to be."

Russell Martin followed with a clutch double on a 2-2 slider that landed on the warning track in left-center, putting the visitors ahead 3-2. Enrique Hernandez connected on a 1-2 slider for yet another two-run double to left-center, a hit off the base off the wall.

After Muncy was intentionally walked, Wander Suero entered and promptly served up a full-count fastball that Justin Turner lofted to the back of the visiting bullpen beyond left field, making it 8-2. The rout was on.

"Just couldn't seem to get that third out there," Corbin said. "It just stinks. I feel like I let these guys down."

And to think: Things were not looking all that good for the Dodgers, who entered the sixth trailing 2-1 after Juan Soto's two-run homer off eventual winner Hyun-Jin Ryu in the first.

Nationals manager Dave Martinez's postseason penchant for pushing his

OPPOSITE: Juan Soto, right, celebrates with Adam Eaton after hitting a two-run home run off Dodgers starting pitcher Hyun-Jin Ryu.
SUSAN WALSH / AP PHOTO

starters to appear in relief continued, deemed necessary because of his club's NL-worst bullpen. The strategy had been working.

"Anibal was at 87 pitches. He gave us all he had. We were at a good spot in the lineup, where we thought Corbin could get through it," Martinez said. "And his stuff was good. ... he had every hitter 0-2. He just couldn't finish."

Martinez has made it clear that he trusts six pitchers on his roster: Scherzer, Strasburg, Corbin, Sánchez and relievers Daniel Hudson and Sean Doolittle. That's why Martinez brought in Scherzer for the eighth inning of Game 2. And that's why Corbin became the latest starter to moonlight in the bullpen.

"You don't have that time to set your pitches up going into it," catcher Yan Gomes said of Corbin making a relief appearance instead of starting. "They already knew what we were going with, and they had some really good at-bats against us."

ABOVE: Anibal Sanchez struck out nine Dodgers in his five innings of work.
PABLO MARTINEZ MONSIVAIS / AP PHOTO

LEFT: Adam Eaton just misses catching a third inning double hit by the Dodgers Justin Turner.
SUSAN WALSH / AP PHOTO

OPPOSITE: Howie Kendrick is tagged out by Dodgers third baseman Justin Turner during the sixth inning.
SUSAN WALSH / AP PHOTO

Scherzer, Zimmerman Lead Way as Nats Force Game 5

WASHINGTON — Max Scherzer is 35. So is Ryan Zimmerman.

The Washington Nationals would not be headed to a win-or-go-home Game 5 in their NL Division Series against the Los Angeles Dodgers without them.

"We're a bunch of viejos. We're old guys," Scherzer joked. "Old guys can still do it."

Sure can. And for a guy whose teams used to lose repeatedly in the postseason, Scherzer sure is delivering now.

Every time he's pitched this October, the Nationals have won. His latest outing was a season-saving, seven-inning masterpiece that combined with Zimmerman's three-run parabola of a homer to lift the wild-card Nationals to a 6-1 victory over league-best Los Angeles, tying the best-of-five NLDS at two games apiece.

"I was just gassed. I was out," said Scherzer, who threw 109 pitches. "I was empty in the tank."

Scowling and muttering to himself as showers fell for part of his gritty performance, Scherzer allowed one run and four hits while striking out nine — and, most importantly for Washington, he prevented LA from closing out the NLDS after taking a 2-1 lead into Game 4.

"He really gave it all he had," said Anthony Rendon, who drove in three runs for Washington.

With fans who braved rain chanting, "Beat LA!" in the late going, Sean Doolittle and Daniel Hudson combined to get the last six outs for Washington.

Zimmerman showed what he still can do at the plate by taking a 97 mph pitch, the second thrown by reliever Pedro Báez, and turning it into a high-arching 400-foot-plus rainbow that descended onto the green batter's eye in straightaway center field for a three-run shot that made it 5-1.

"Zim put a really good swing on it," Dodgers manager Dave Roberts said.

That was after Julio Urías, LA's third pitcher and the one charged with the loss, began the fifth by serving up a line-drive single to Trea Turner, who finished with three hits. Rendon, who led the majors with 126 RBIs during the regular season but entered Monday with just one in the playoffs, delivered a run-scoring single that made it 2-1.

Rendon also brought home runs via sacrifice flies in the third and sixth.

That was plenty for Scherzer, who clenched his teeth while getting through his last inning after loading the bases by issuing a pair of walks with one out in the seventh. But he got out of that by striking out pinch-hitter Chris Taylor and getting Joc Pederson — whose liner on a first-pitch cut landed about an inch foul — to ground out.

Scherzer shook his arms and yelled as he stalked to the home dugout.

OPPOSITE: Joc Pederson (31) strikes out swinging after getting fooled badly on a change-up from Nationals pitcher Max Scherzer.

JULIO CORTEZ / AP PHOTO

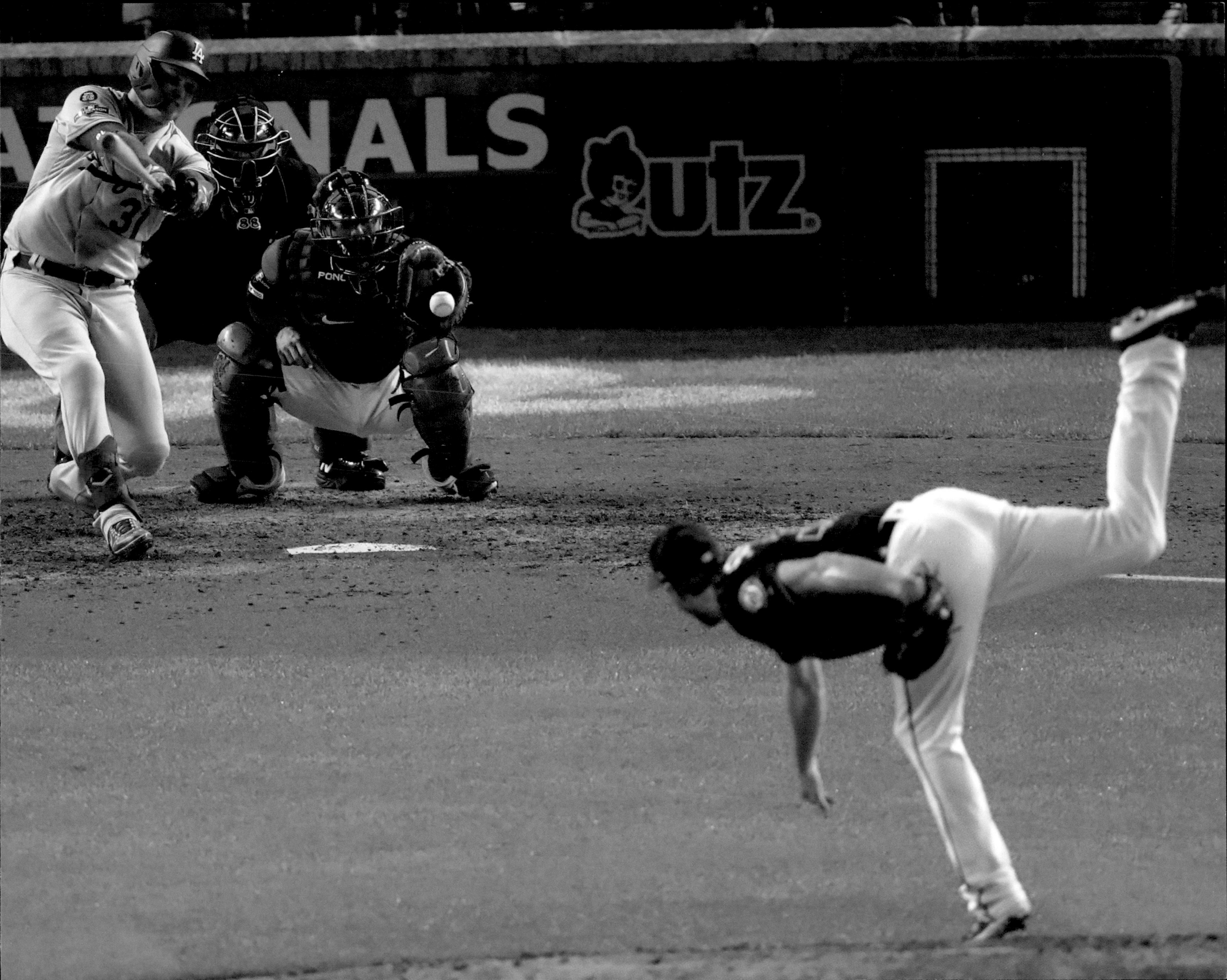
NALS
utz

"You can't say enough about his compete," Roberts said. "He just sort of wills his way to getting outs."

The Dodgers' lone run came when Justin Turner connected for a no-doubt-about-it homer to left on Scherzer's 10th pitch, a 95-mph fastball. But from there, facing an LA lineup stacked with a half-dozen lefty hitters, Scherzer displayed the sort of ornery dominance that helped him win three Cy Young Awards.

"He might look like a maniac out there," catcher Kurt Suzuki said, "but he's smart."

Scherzer said a Game 5 appearance was out of the question.

"That pushed me all the way to the edge and then some tonight," he said. "So, yeah, I can't imagine any scenario where I'm pitching."

Zimmerman for so many years was the face of the franchise for the Nationals, who made him their first draft pick 14 years ago. So he's been through all their highs, including four NL East titles, and lows, including early exit after early exit in the playoffs. He no longer is an everyday player — Game 4 marked his second start of this postseason — and his teammate-mandated dugout dance after his homer consisted of pretending to use a walker.

"He's been here forever," Rendon said. "Man, he means everything to this city, to this team."

This could be a last hurrah for Zimmerman with the Nationals, who hold an $18 million contract option on him in 2020. He insists he's not thinking about the future, other than figuring that he'll continue playing beyond this season.

"There's been a lot of people," Zimmerman said, "that think these are my last games."

That prompted Scherzer to pipe up.

"I really don't think," Scherzer said, "these are his last games."

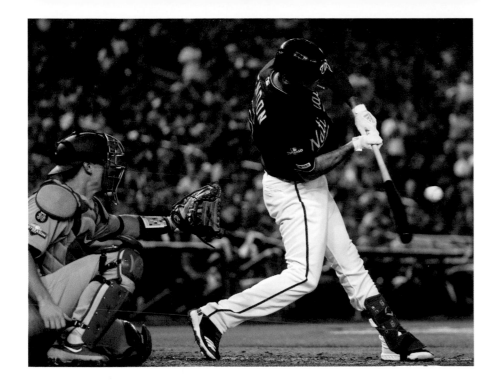

UPPER LEFT: Anthony Rendon hits an RBI-single off Dodgers relief pitcher Julio Urias during the fifth inning.
ALEX BRANDON / AP PHOTO

ABOVE: Starting pitcher Max Scherzer, right, is greeted by teammates in the dugout after pitching seven strong innings.
ALEX BRANDON / AP PHOTO

LEFT: Ryan Zimmerman hits a three-run home run off Dodgers relief pitcher Pedro Baez (52) in the fifth inning.
JULIO CORTEZ / AP PHOTO

OPPOSITE: Trea Turner slides safely in to third base ahead of the tag by the Dodgers Justin Turner.
TONY QUINN / AP PHOTO

Nats Stun Dodgers on Kendrick's 10th-inning Slam

LOS ANGELES — Howie Kendrick and the Washington Nationals got down again but were never out -- and they finally ended their streak of playoff series futility in grand fashion.

Kendrick hit a tiebreaking grand slam in the 10th inning and the Nationals, boosted by a lightning rally against Clayton Kershaw, beat the Los Angeles Dodgers 7-3 Wednesday night in Game 5. They advanced to the NL Championship Series starting Friday at St. Louis.

"I was hoping for any moment," said Kendrick, a 36-year-old veteran who was hitless in his first four at-bats.

In their first season since star slugger Bryce Harper left as a free agent, the Nationals became the first team in major league history to rally from three or more runs down twice in elimination games during the same postseason.

"It's not just one player, it's a team," left fielder Juan Soto said.

The wild-card Nationals won a playoff series for the first time since the team moved to Washington ahead of the 2005 season, and the franchise reached the NLCS for the second time in 51 seasons.

"Oh, man, keep fighting," Anthony Rendon said. "I think that's the story of maybe this organization."

Rendon and Soto homered on consecutive pitches to overcome a 3-1 deficit in the eighth against Kershaw, a three-time Cy Young Award winner. Soto had started the comeback from a 3-0 hole with an RBI single in the sixth off starter Walker Buehler and then hit a 449-foot drive halfway up the right-field pavilion off Kershaw, the longest home run of the 20-year-old's big league career.

Adam Eaton walked against Joe Kelly leading off the 10th, Rendon doubled on a drive that lodged in the left-field wall and Soto was intentionally walked.

Kendrick was 4 for 19 with one RBI in the series and had made a pair of errors at first base in the Game 1 loss. He fouled off a pitch and then hit a 97-mph fastball over the wall in dead center for his second career slam.

"It was electric. Probably the best moment of my career," said Kendrick, a 14-year big league veteran. "We never gave up. The city had faith in us. The fans had faith in us. We believed in ourselves, everybody came through for us."

Dodgers fans started exiting as the bases emptied, realizing their team's streak of NLCS appearances would not reach four.

"Disappointing is probably an understatement," manager Dave Roberts said.

Daniel Hudson got the win, retiring Will Smith on a drive to the right field warning track with one on and one out in the ninth, then getting Chris Taylor on a liner to center.

Sean Doolittle pitched a perfect 10th for Washington, with center fielder

OPPOSITE: Howie Kendrick (47) watches his grand slam off Dodgers relief pitcher Joe Kelly leave the park during the top of the 10th inning.

MARK J. TERRILL / AP PHOTO

dodgers.com/memberships
DODGERS.COM
Dodgers
17
Nationals
47
ALL-STAR GAME
HOME OF THE

Michael A. Taylor making a diving catch on Justin Turner for the final out.

"I'm really excited for the boys in that clubhouse that fought all year," Nationals manager Dave Martinez said.

Kershaw sat on the bench after the home runs, looking forlorn, bowing his head and holding it in his hands. He has a 4.43 ERA in 32 postseason appearances, nearly double his superb 2.44 ERA over a dozen regular seasons.

"Everything people say is true right now about the postseason," Kershaw said.

The left-hander had replaced Buehler with two on and two outs in the seventh, and struck out Eaton on three pitches. Roberts didn't hesitate to stay with Kershaw in the eighth.

"He's probably the best pitcher of our generation," Roberts said. "It just didn't work out. There's always going to be second-guessing. I'll take my chances any day with Clayton."

Washington's Stephen Strasburg fell behind 2-0 after eight pitches. Joc Pederson doubled on a drive that went through an opening in the left-field wall -- the crowd saw it land in the seats and thought it was a home run——but he was awarded the double after a video review. Max Muncy, who had been 0 for 12 against Strasburg, drove a fastball over the center-field wall.

Kike Hernandez homered on Strasburg's second pitch of the second inning, another fastball, for a 3-0 lead.

Strasburg gave up three runs and six hits in six innings, struck out seven and walked one.

Buehler allowed one run and four hits in 6 2/3 innings before Kershaw came in.

There was a scary moment when Buehler hit Kurt Suzuki on the left wrist and the ball shot up and knocked off his helmet as the ballpark went silent. Suzuki fell to the ground, grabbing his face. He walked off his under his own power and was replaced by Yan Gomes, who moved behind the plate in the bottom half.

ABOVE: Howie Kendrick (47) celebrates with teammates Ryan Zimmerman (11), Anthony Rendon (6) and Juan Soto (22) after hitting a grand slam to advance the Nats to the NLCS.
MARK J. TERRILL / AP PHOTO

OPPOSITE: Juan Soto celebrates his eighth inning home run.
MARK J. TERRILL / AP PHOTO

71

ABOVE: Sean Doolittle, left, leaps into the arms of catcher Yan Gomes after getting the final out in the Nationals 7-3 win.
MARCIO JOSE SANCHEZ / AP PHOTO

FAR LEFT: Manager Dave Martinez gets a champagne shower as he celebrates with his team in the locker room.
MARCIO JOSE SANCHEZ / AP PHOTO

LEFT: The Nationals celebrate their win.
MARCIO JOSE SANCHEZ / AP PHOTO

OPPOSITE: In a scary moment during the seventh inning, Kurt Suzuki gets hit by a pitch that ricocheted off his left wrist knocking off his helmet. Suzuki fell to the ground, but was able to walk off under his own power.
MARK J. TERRILL / AP PHOTO

Sánchez Shines in NLCS Opener

ST. LOUIS — It turns out Washington's Big Three is a Big Four. Don't forget about Anibal Sanchez.

The right-hander carried a no-hit bid into the eighth inning, Howie Kendrick had two more big swings and the Nationals beat the St. Louis Cardinals 2-0 in the NL Championship Series opener.

"Tonight was obviously vintage Anibal," first baseman Ryan Zimmerman said.

Sanchez had allowed just three runners when he took the mound for the eighth. Zimmerman robbed Tommy Edman with an outstanding diving grab at full stretch for the first out, but pinch-hitter Jose Martinez cleanly singled to center with two down for the Cardinals' first hit.

"I just tried to keep focused on every pitch that I'm going to throw," Sanchez said. "I don't want to miss any kind of pitch in the middle in the zone against those guys."

Sanchez thought he was going to finish the no-hitter after the big grab.

"When Zimmerman caught that ball I said, 'OK, always behind a no-hitter, a good play has to happen,'" Sanchez said. "I said, OK, I [have] it."

Sean Doolittle relieved and got four straight outs to finish the one-hitter for his first postseason save in two years.

Sanchez and Doolittle made life easy on manager Dave Martinez after the Nationals placed closer Daniel Hudson on the paternity list before the franchise's first appearance in the NLCS since the Montreal Expos moved to Washington ahead of the 2005 season.

"I think the mood of the guys in the bullpen, we really wanted to find a way to pick him up and allow him to enjoy a really special moment with his wife and his family," Doolittle said.

"People were talking about the Big Three," Cardinals manager Mike Shildt said, "but we got a guy tonight that we got to contend with and not overlook him."

St. Louis wasted a solid performance by Miles Mikolas, who pitched six innings of one-run ball in his second career playoff start.

Washington scored each of its runs with two outs. Kendrick doubled and came home on Yan Gomes' double in the second. Kendrick then singled in Adam Eaton in the seventh after Eaton reached on a one-out triple against Giovanny Gallegos.

"It's going to be a fun series," Kendrick said. "Hopefully we can continue to play really good baseball and put up runs and get some wins."

Gomes finished with two hits while subbing for catcher Kurt Suzuki, who left the Nationals' clinching victory against the Dodgers with a head injury.

Sanchez became the first pitcher to start two postseason games with six hitless

OPPOSITE: Anibal Sanchez throws during the first inning of Game 1 of the NLCS.
MARK HUMPHREY / AP PHOTO

Max's Masterpiece

Nats take 2-0 NLCS lead

ST. LOUIS — Max Scherzer was strength and fire. Aníbal Snchez was artistry and deception.

Two different styles, two absolute gems for the Washington Nationals.

Scherzer followed Sánchez's near no-hitter with a try of his own, and the stingy Nationals beat the St. Louis Cardinals 3-1 for a 2-0 lead in the NL Championship Series.

"We really want to win here," the hard-charging Scherzer said. "So that's what's going to happen, we're going to compete and win."

Scherzer didn't allow a hit until Paul Goldschmidt led off the seventh inning with a single that left fielder Juan Soto played conservatively with a 1-0 lead. A day earlier, Sánchez held the Cardinals hitless until José Martínez had a pinch single with two down in the eighth.

Only once in postseason history had teammates held an opponent hitless through the first five innings in consecutive games. That was in 2013, when Sánchez and Scherzer, then with the Tigers, held the Red Sox hitless in the first two games of the ALCS.

Now they've done it again.

"The way he can change speeds and execute pitches, it's a treat to really watch and get to pitch with him," Scherzer said. "For me, I'm just in the moment. I'm not trying to do anything great, I'm just trying to stick within my game."

Scherzer, a St. Louis native who played college ball for the University of Missouri, struck out 11 and walked two in seven innings.

"Typical," shortstop Trea Turner said. "He's been really good for a long time, no matter the situation, the opponent, whatever it may be. He's been really good, and he was really good again today."

It doesn't get any easier for St. Louis, either. Ace Stephen Strasburg gets the ball for the wild-card Nationals when the best-of-seven series moves to Washington for Game 3.

"They have a pretty strong advantage right now," Cardinals right-hander Adam Wainwright said.

"I've got a lot of confidence in our hitters. I think our hitters are going to do something special in Washington."

St. Louis got another solid performance from Wainwright, who struck out 11 in 7 1/3 innings.

But after getting only one hit in the opener, the Cardinals' inconsistent lineup managed just three hits against Scherzer and the Washington bullpen.

"We trust in each other. We've been in this position before," Cardinals catcher Yadier Molina said. "We just have to figure out how to get better."

OPPOSITE: Max Scherzer unleashes a fast ball during fourth inning action.
MARK HUMPHREY / AP PHOTO

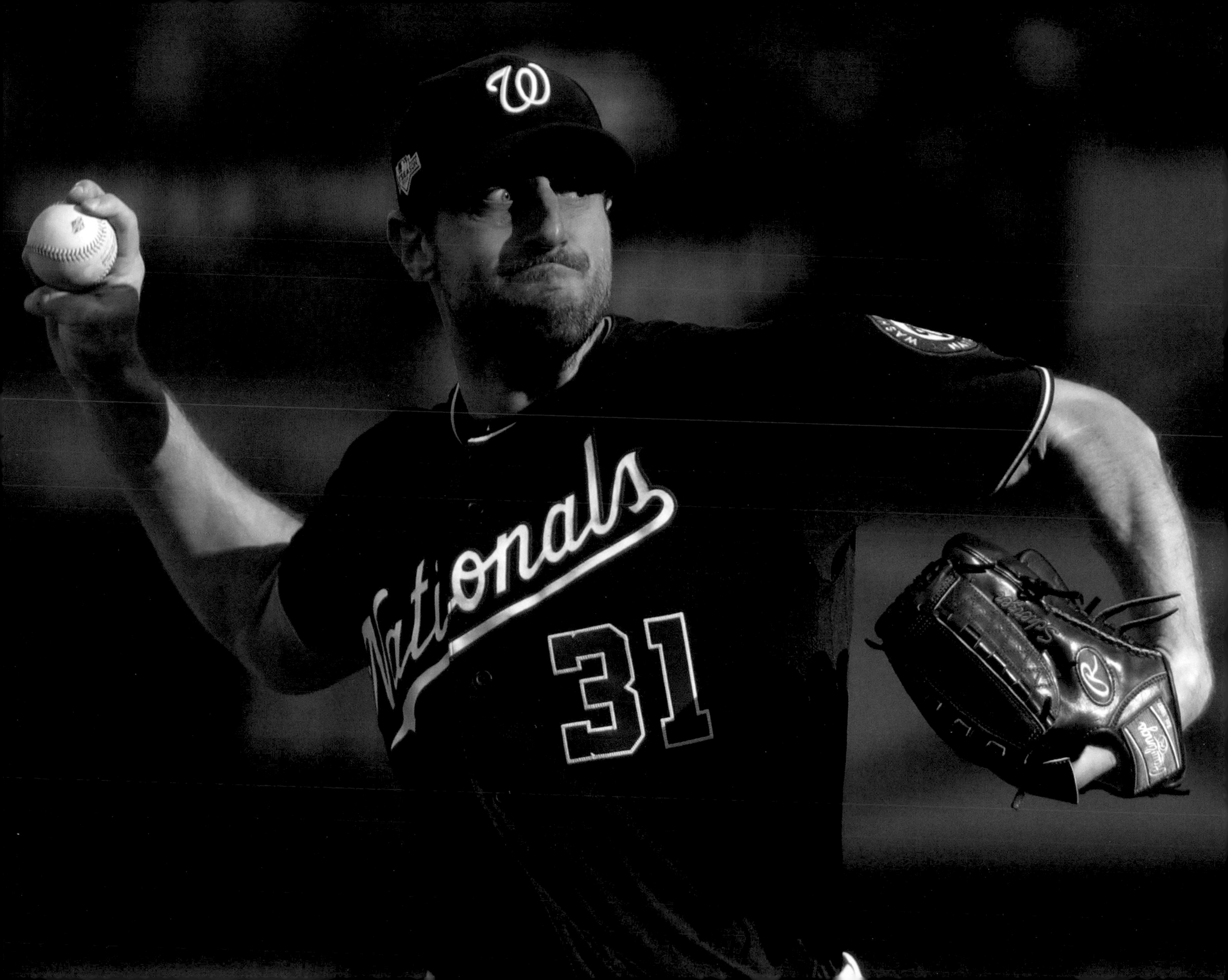
Nationals
31

ABOVE: Juan Soto (22), Adam Eaton (2) and Michael A. Taylor (3) celebrate after Game 2.
JEFF ROBERSON / AP PHOTO

MIDDLE: Pinch hitter Matt Adams connects for a single during the top of the eighth inning.
JEFF ROBERSON / AP PHOTO

RIGHT: Adam Eaton goes up high to catch a ball hit by the Cardinals Tommy Edman during the eighth inning.
JEFF ROBERSON / AP PHOTO

The NL Central champions got their first run of the series when center fielder Michael A. Taylor misplayed Martínez's pinch-hit liner into an RBI double with two outs in the eighth. But Dexter Fowler flied out on Sean Doolittle's next pitch on a tough day to see the ball with the shadows from the mid-afternoon start.

Patrick Corbin got the first out of the ninth before Daniel Hudson earned his third save of the playoffs. The right-hander was reinstated from the postseason paternity list before the game after he missed the series opener to be with his wife, Sara, for the birth of their third child, a girl named Millie.

Scherzer, who has pitched two no-hitters in the regular season, has a record five career postseason no-hit bids of at least five innings, according to the Elias Sports Bureau. The three-time Cy Young Award winner came closest to finishing in Game 3 of the 2017 NL Division Series, getting one out in the seventh inning before allowing a hit.

"It's a good ballclub, but we've got great pitchers," Taylor said. "They went out and executed pitch after pitch."

The Cardinals got one baserunner into scoring position while Scherzer was on the mound. Kolten Wong walked with one out in the first and stole second, but Goldschmidt and Marcell Ozuna struck out.

After Goldschmidt's hit, Ozuna struck out again and Molina bounced into an inning-ending double play on Scherzer's final pitch of the afternoon.

Washington went ahead to stay when Taylor homered on Wainwright's first pitch of the third. The Nationals added two more on Adam Eaton's double down the first-base line with one out in the eighth.

"It's not just one guy carrying this team or two guys," Scherzer said. "It's really just a collective of everybody out there doing their job."

Howie Kendrick makes a tough play on a ground ball hit by the Cardinals Kolten Wong during the fourth inning.
JEFF ROBERSON / AP PHOTO

Strasburg Ks 12, Nats One Win from World Series

WASHINGTON — More than 100 pitches in, Stephen Strasburg was adamant he wasn't quite ready to leave the latest superb start by a Nationals pitcher against the St. Louis Cardinals in the NL Championship Series -- a win that put Washington on the verge of the city's first World Series in 86 years.

It was the seventh inning, and manager Dave Martinez noticed Strasburg had flexed his right leg and reached for that hamstring. So the skipper and a trainer went to the mound to check on their guy.

"I was trying to explain to him, `Hey, you just grabbed your hamstring, so there's a little concern," Martinez recalled. "He said, `No, I cramped up. It's fine. I always cramp up.' He said, `I'm staying in the game. I want to finish this inning.' I said, `You sure you're all right?' He said, `I'm in the game!'"

The right-hander did, indeed, stay in. Even struck out the next two batters to raise his total to 12 Ks, each finished with an off-speed pitch. Strasburg took his turn silencing the Cardinals' struggling bats, Nationals postseason star Howie Kendrick doubled three times and drove in three more runs, and Washington took a 3-0 lead in the best-of-seven NLCS by beating St. Louis 8-1.

"It's a little surreal," reliever Sean Doolittle said about being one win from the World Series, "and I think that's why it's important that we don't look too far ahead."

After Nationals starters Anibal Sanchez and Max Scherzer flirted with no-hitters in the first two games against the Cardinals, Strasburg wasn't quite that untouchable: He allowed a double in the second inning, six later singles and one unearned run.

Still, the Cardinals, quite simply, can't score in this NLCS: They have a grand total of two runs and 11 hits through three games. Washington's three starters have a combined ERA -- no calculator necessary for this one -- of 0.00.

Yes, that's zero-point-zero-zero.

"We expected better," said Kolten Wong, who went 0 for 4 on Monday and is 0 for 10 in the series for St. Louis.

Now it's Patrick Corbin's chance to see if he can match his rotation-mates. The $140 million lefty will start for the Nationals in Game 4 on Tuesday night, when they can close out a sweep at home.

"We've got to get a lead at some point in this series. Hard to win a game if you can't get a lead," St. Louis manager Mike Shildt said. "We've got to figure out a way to create some offense early in the game and be able to hold it there."

Washington hasn't put a baseball team in the World Series since 1933, when the Senators lost to the New York Giants in five games. The nation's capital owns only one MLB championship; the Senators won all the way back in 1924.

OPPOSITE: Victor Robles soaks in the fans cheers after hitting a sixth inning home run.
JEFF ROBERSON / AP PHOTO

Until this season, the Nationals hadn't won a playoff series, going 0-4 since 2012, but they sure look as if they're making up for lost time.

"Shoot, maybe we're finally coming around," third baseman Anthony Rendon said.

How about this current run? The Nationals, who found themselves at 19-31 in late May, have won 15 of their past 17 games, stretching back to the last week of the regular season.

It all starts with the pitching.

"That's what our team is built around. You have those guys, those horses, that take the ball every fifth day," said Ryan Zimmerman, who drove in two runs. "They haven't disappointed, obviously, in the postseason, but they've kind of been the backbone of this team all year."

Against Sanchez in Game 1, the first hit for the Cardinals arrived with their 27th batter. Against Scherzer in Game 2, it was their 21st batter. But even when the Cardinals did something right against Strasburg, they erased it by doing something wrong.

Their fourth batter, Marcell Ozuna, doubled to the left field corner in the second, then quickly erased himself with some poor baserunning, going too far toward third on a comebacker and getting tagged out by Strasburg, who is enjoying a postseason to remember.

Much to the delight of a red towel-twirling crowd of 43,675, Washington's batters kept delivering, led by Kendrick, who has eight RBI in the past four games.

The Nationals roughed up Jack Flaherty for four runs, all in the third inning; he hadn't allowed that many in a game since July 2, a span of 18 appearances.

Seven of Washington's eight runs came with two outs, and there were contributions from up and down the lineup: Victor Robles homered in his return from a hamstring injury, and Rendon heard "MVP!" chants after a slick defensive play and an RBI double.

The Nationals Adam Eaton races around to score on a third inning double by Anthony Rendon.

TOP: Strasburg was dominant all day with 12 Ks in seven innings.

LOWER: Relief pitcher Fernando Rodney rides in from the bullpen in style for an eighth inning appearance.

TOP: Howie Kendrick crushes a double during the seventh inning. He would score on Ryan Zimmerman's base hit.

LOWER: The Presidents Race during the fourth inning.

A Clean Sweep

Nationals head to first World Series in 86 years

WASHINGTON — As the Washington Nationals moved a party 86 years in the making from their ballpark's infield to a booze-filled clubhouse, manager Dave Martinez paused near the dugout and thrust the silver NL Championship Series trophy overhead, to the delight of loud, delirious fans still in the stands.

Who would have thought this was possible five months ago, when the team was flailing, trade talk was swirling around Washington and folks figured Martinez's job was in jeopardy?

From 19-31 during a mediocre May to the Fall Classic in an outstanding October -- and the city's first World Series appearance since 1933.

Extending their stunning turnaround, the wild-card Nationals got RBI from middle-of-the-order stars Anthony Rendon and Juan Soto in a seven-run first inning, and Patrick Corbin's 12-strikeout performance plus a trio of relievers helped hold on to beat the St. Louis Cardinals 7-4 in Game 4 to complete a sweep in the NLCS.

"Often, bumpy roads lead to beautiful places," said Martinez, who underwent a heart procedure in September, "and this is a beautiful place."

Right from the first inning, most in a sellout crowd of 43,976 rose from their seats to applaud or yell or twirl their red towels, to chant "Let's go, Nats!" and "M-V-P!" and various players' names, enjoying every moment of that game-deciding outburst.

And then, a couple of hours and several innings later, as Tanner Rainey, Sean Doolittle and Daniel Hudson were protecting a shrinking lead, those same spectators stood and shouted and reveled some more.

"I just kept counting down: We're 12 outs from the World Series. We're nine outs from the World Series, six, three," shortstop Trea Turner said.

Now the Nationals get plenty of time to rest and set up their so-far terrific rotation before beginning the last series of the season in a week.

"We think we can compete with any team, any time," NLCS MVP Howie Kendrick said. "People always get caught up in the things that are on paper, but the reality of it is you have to go out and play. Once we get out on the field, anything can happen."

The last time the World Series came to the nation's capital, more than eight decades ago, the Washington Senators lost to the New York Giants in five

OPPOSITE: Yan Gomes and Daniel Hudson hug after getting the final out in the Nationals sweep of the St. Louis Cardinals.

PATRICK SEMANSKY / AP PHOTO

games. Have to go even further back, to 1924, for the city's lone baseball championship, when the Senators defeated the Giants.

The Senators eventually left, and the town didn't have a major league team at all for more than three decades until the Montreal Expos -- who were founded in 1969 and never made it to the World Series -- moved to Washington in 2005.

The Nationals had never managed to advance in the postseason since arriving, going 0-4 in the NLDS over the last seven years, including three Game 5 losses at home.

First baseman Ryan Zimmerman, the Nationals' first draft pick in Washington, was there for all of that heartache.

"Sometimes," he said, "you got to wait for good things."

This month alone, the Nationals beat the Milwaukee Brewers in the NL wild-card game after trailing 3-1 heading to the eighth, and eliminated the league-best Los Angeles Dodgers in Game 5 of the NL Division Series after trailing 3-1 heading to the eighth again.

Then came this lopsided dismissal of the NL Central champion Cardinals, who were outscored 20-6 in the series.

Corbin, a left-handed pitcher signed with $140 million of the money that became available last offseason when Bryce Harper left town to join the Philadelphia Phillies, was not quite the equal of Washington's other starters in the series.

Still, he did become the first pitcher to strike out 10 batters in the first four innings of a postseason game and earned the win after allowing four runs in five innings.

Then Martinez turned to his NL-worst bullpen, such a problem for so much of this season.

After Rainey got three outs, and Doolittle got five, Hudson came in for his fourth save in four chances this postseason. It wasn't easy, though: After replacing Doolittle with two outs in the eighth, Hudson hit his first batter and walked his second, bringing pinch-hitter Matt Carpenter to the plate as the go-ahead run with the bases loaded.

Carpenter, a career .481 batter with the bases full, grounded out to second baseman Brian Dozier, a defensive replacement who briefly lost the ball before gathering it and throwing to first to end that inning.

Hudson finished things with a perfect ninth, getting Tommy Edman on a fly ball to center field to end it, and red fireworks went off around the stadium.

TOP: Ryan Zimmerman and Howie Kendrick celebrate after scoring on a Yan Gomes base hit in the bottom of the first inning.
JEFF ROBERSON / AP PHOTO

RIGHT: Trea Turner drives in two giving the Nats a 7-0 lead in the bottom of the first inning.
ALEX BRANDON / AP PHOTO

TOP LEFT: Yan Gomes and Daniel Hudson celebrate after Game 4.
JEFF ROBERSON / AP PHOTO

ABOVE: Nationals manager Dave Martinez kisses the National League Championship Trophy.
JEFF ROBERSON / AP PHOTO

LEFT: The National League Champion Washington Nationals.
JEFF ROBERSON / AP PHOTO

The Old Guys Help Nationals Make Series

NL MVP candidate Anthony Rendon surveyed his teammates scattered around the Nationals Park diamond, whoopin' it up after clinching a World Series berth.

There were starting pitchers Max Scherzer and Aníbal Sánchez, each 35 — and each responsible for taking a no-hit bid into at least the seventh inning as Washington won Games 1 and 2 of the NL Championship Series. So was Howie Kendrick, 36, the second baseman who earned NLCS MVP honors with four doubles and four RBIs in the sweep. And Ryan Zimmerman, 35, the first baseman slugging .484 this postseason.

"A lot of old guys on the team," Rendon observed. "They call themselves 'Viejos.'"

Indeed, they do, and "Los Viejos" — Spanish for "The Old Guys" — are a big part of why the Nationals are getting ready to face the Astros in the Fall Classic.

There's also catcher Kurt Suzuki, 36, and reliever Fernando Rodney, 42, the oldest active player in the majors.

"People think we are old men and we can't do things," said Rodney, who credited Suzuki with originating the nickname. "So we say, 'Vamos, Viejos! You can do it!'"

They helped make Washington the oldest club in baseball in 2019, with an average age of a tad under 31.

The Astros aren't exactly spring chickens, either: With an average age of just above 30, they ranked third oldest out of Major League Baseball's 30 clubs. Just like the Nationals, their roster includes a half-dozen players who are at least 35, including rotation stalwarts Justin Verlander and Zack Greinke.

Astros star Alex Bregman has noticed.

"I know how they say let the kids play," the 25-year-old third baseman said Monday. "But there are some veterans that can show the kids how to play."

Makes sense to Suzuki.

"Older players sometimes get devalued a little bit, just because of the age," he said. "You can call us old, but that's fine. We don't care. We feel like we can still contribute and we can still play at a high level. And I think that's the only thing that matters."

Scherzer, for example, is a three-time Cy Young Award winner who followed up yet another stellar regular season by compiling a 1.80 ERA in four appearances in the playoffs; Washington went 4-0 in those games.

Sánchez has made two starts this postseason with a 0.71 ERA.

Like Scherzer and Sánchez, Rodney is one of a half-dozen members of the Nationals to already have appeared in a World Series (only one, little-used reliever Hunter Strickland, has won a title).

Rodney has been a key part of the late-season rebirth of the team's bullpen: He has allowed two hits and zero runs in 2 2/3 innings in the playoffs.

"I look at them, and they're not old to me," 55-year-old manager Dave Martinez said. "They're playing like I've seen them play when they were 27, 28."

Sure, the Nationals do have a couple of kids playing key roles in starting outfielders Juan Soto, 20, and Victor Robles, 22. But there's not much else at that end of the spectrum, which is why when second baseman Brian Dozier, 32, was asked what advice he's giving the younger guys, he chuckled and responded: "Younger guys? You mean the two that's in here?"

Dozier thinks it's important to have a lot of veterans at this time of year — players who have been around are used to dealing with distractions such as an increased media presence and have a better grasp of how to, as he put it, "slow the game down a lot more" when the pressure increases.

"The chemistry and the experience that veteran guys bring, you can't put that into an algorithm. You can't put a money value on it. So people don't like it. But there's definitely a place for those guys," Zimmerman said. "You can't have a team filled with old guys, either. Nobody's saying that. I'm just saying that there are spots on every team for veteran guys who have been there and done that and have experience and can teach the young, talented guys that are basically going to carry the game on to the next generation how to respect the game, how to play the game the right way."

Nationals GM Mike Rizzo likes the way the older players mentor the younger ones.

He also likes the production "Los Viejos" provide.

"We knew we were the oldest team in the league, and everybody said that's a negative. We just tried to flip that and made it a positive, because we know how good … we can still play. All of us, even the old guys," Scherzer said. "For me, I don't even feel old. I feel young. I feel great and know that I can go out there and do everything I could do back when I was 25 years old."

LEFT: Fernando Rodney
MATT SLOCUM / AP PHOTO

TOP: Anibal Sanchez
DUANE BURLESON / AP PHOTO

ABOVE: Max Scherzer, left, and catcher Kurt Suzuki, right.
DUANE BURLESON / AP PHOTO

Soto Strikes First, Nats take 1-0 World Series Lead

HOUSTON — Juan Soto and the Washington Nationals quickly derailed the Cole Express.

A 20-year-old prodigy with a passion for the big moment, Soto homered onto the train tracks high above the left field wall and hit a two-run double as the Nationals tagged Gerrit Cole and the Houston Astros in the World Series opener.

"After the first at-bat, I just said, 'It's another baseball game,'" Soto said. "In the first at-bat, I'm not going to lie, I was a little bit shaking in my legs."

Not even a history-making home run by postseason star George Springer — and another shot that nearly tied it in the eighth inning — could deter Washington.

Ryan Zimmerman, still full of sock at 35, also homered to back a resourceful Max Scherzer and boost the wild-card Nationals in their first World Series appearance — tres bien for a franchise that began as the Montreal Expos in 1969.

"They waited a long time," Nationals manager Dave Martinez said.

Otherworldly almost all season, Cole looked downright ordinary. Trea Turner singled on the second pitch of the game and the Nationals were off and running, ending Cole's 19-game winning streak that stretched back 25 starts to May.

"I didn't have my A-game tonight," Cole said.

Not what Cole or anyone else at Minute Maid Park expected, especially after he led the majors in strikeouts, topped the AL in ERA and finished second in the big leagues in wins to teammate Justin Verlander.

Cole had breezed through the AL playoffs, too.

Yet it was a further testament to an eternal truth about baseball: It doesn't matter what you do the whole season if you don't get it done in October.

"I think he's been so good for so long that there builds this thought of invincibility and that it's impossible to beat him," Astros manager AJ Hinch said. "So when it happens it is a surprise to all of us."

Soto finished with three hits and a stolen base. Three days shy of his 21st birthday, the wunderkind left fielder also snared Michael Brantley's late try for a tying hit.

Relentless at the plate, he's already become one of those rare players — like Springer — who seems to turn pressure into production.

How's he do it? Better launch angle? Improved swing path?

Uh, not really.

"Sometimes I just put gum in my mouth," Soto said. "But most of the time, just take a deep breath and focus. It's just the pitcher and me."

The MVP when Houston won its first crown in 2017, Springer set a record by

OPPOSITE: Juan Soto crushes a fourth inning home to tie the game at 2-2.
DAVID J. PHILLIP / AP PHOTO

connecting in his fifth straight Series game to make it 5-3 in the seventh. But reliever Daniel Hudson threw a fastball past rookie Yordan Álvarez with the bases loaded to end the inning.

In the eighth, Springer put a charge into a drive to deep right-center, and it appeared as though he might've hit a tying, two-run homer. Springer took a couple of hops out of the batter's box to watch, and had to settle for an RBI double when the ball glanced off the glove of a leaping Adam Eaton at the fence.

Scherzer slipped in and out of trouble for five innings. But every time the stadium got rollicking, he found a way to get out of jams. There's a reason ol' Max has won three Cy Young Awards.

"We got old and young guys," Scherzer said.

Projected Game 4 starter Patrick Corbin threw a scoreless sixth for the Nationals. Springer connected off Tanner Rainey for his 14th career postseason home

ABOVE: Anthony Rendon celebrates in the dugout after scoring on a double by Juan Soto during the fifth inning.
MATT SLOCUM / AP PHOTO

FAR LEFT: Ryan Zimmerman gets the Nats on the board with a second inning home run.
ERIC GAY / AP PHOTO

LEFT: Soto does his baby shark gesture towards the Nats dugout after hitting a double in the fifth inning.
DAVID J. PHILLIP / AP PHOTO

run before Hudson fanned Álvarez on three pitches.

Hudson retired José Altuve, and Sean Doolittle got Brantley on a lineout to strand Springer at second in the eighth. Doolittle then closed for a save to give the Nationals their seventh straight victory and 17th in 19 games dating to their September playoff run.

Leading the way was Soto, whose eighth-inning hit in the wild-card win over Milwaukee sent the Nationals on their path.

"He's got kind of the 'it' factor," Hinch said. "He's got the twitch. He's got fast hands. He's got no fear."

Soto looked overmatched when he fanned on Cole's 99 mph heater in the first inning. Turned out Soto was just getting warmed up.

He justified his place in the 4-spot, launching a leadoff drive in the fourth to make it 2-all. The ball was later retrieved from the train tracks and donated by Soto for a long ride to the Hall of Fame in Cooperstown.

Washington took the lead in the fifth. Eaton hit a tiebreaking single and Soto doubled with two outs for a 5-2 advantage.

After the game, Soto agreed to donate his home run ball to the Hall of Fame in Cooperstown.

Zimmerman hit the first World Series homer in Nationals history, connecting in the second. He was the first player drafted by the team for the 2005 season.

"It's been a long ride," Zimmerman said.

RIGHT: Adam Eaton can't get a glove on a RBI-double by the Astros George Springer during the eighth inning.
MATT SLOCUM / AP PHOTO

OPPOSITE: The Nationals celebrate after their Game 1 win.
MATT SLOCUM / AP PHOTO

Capital Punishment

Nats pound Astros for 2-0 Series lead

HOUSTON — Stephen Strasburg's time had come.

Famously held out of the postseason seven years ago, Strasburg delivered on the biggest stage of all Wednesday night.

The right-hander outdueled fellow ace Justin Verlander, overcoming a shaky start to give the Washington Nationals a 12-3 win over the Houston Astros and a commanding 2-0 lead in the World Series.

Kurt Suzuki hit a tiebreaking homer in what became a messy six-run seventh inning, and the Nationals headed back home to Washington for three games — if needed.

"He's a guy who always gets big hits," Nationals veteran Ryan Zimmerman said of Suzuki.

Adam Eaton paraded around the bases pointing to the Houston crowd after a late home run as the Nationals won their eighth in a row. They've won 18 of 20 overall dating back to the regular season, with the last two over AL Cy Young Award favorites Gerrit Cole and Verlander.

Game 3 is Friday night when Aníbal Sánchez opposes Houston's Zack Greinke in the first World Series game in the nation's capital since 1933.

The 31-year-old Strasburg had waited years for this chance. Back in 2012, he was about two years removed from Tommy John surgery when Nationals brass decided protecting his elbow was more important than pitching him in the playoffs, so he was shut down late in a season full of promise.

Making his Series debut, Strasburg allowed a two-run homer to Alex Bregman in the first before throwing five shutout innings to improve 4-0 this postseason. He allowed seven hits and struck out seven.

A likely Hall of Famer with a supermodel wife, the 36-year-old Verlander is 0-5 with a 5.73 ERA in six World Series starts. Never before has a pitcher lost his first five World Series decisions.

He gave up seven hits and four runs, and was lifted after walking a batter following Suzuki's home run.

"When he gives you a pitch to hit you can't miss it," Suzuki said.

Verlander led the majors with 21 wins this season and struck out a career-high 300 to reach 3,000 in his career. He has a World Series ring, MVP and Cy Award trophies, and three no-hitters on his resume.

He struck out six to become the career leader in postseason Ks with 202 — another impressive statistic on a stellar resume that is still missing that elusive World Series win.

Their dominance against Houston's best pitchers turned the underdog Nationals into heavy favorites to win the title. Only three of the previous 25

OPPOSITE: Anthony Rendon drives in two runs with a first inning double.
DAVID J. PHILLIP / AP PHOTO

teams to lose the first two games at home under the 2-3-2 format have come back to win the Series. No one has done it since the 1996 New York Yankees.

Things went wrong immediately for Verlander when he walked leadoff man Trea Turner on four pitches. Eaton, who homered in the eighth, singled before Anthony Rendon knocked a ball off the wall in left field for a double that put the Nationals up 2-0.

Michael Brantley singled with two outs in the bottom of the first before Bregman's homer to left tied it. After hitting .167 with no homers in the ALCS and struggling in the opener of this series, Bregman took a second to admire his homer before nonchalantly tossing his bat and trotting to first.

All eight of Bregman's postseason home runs have come off All-Stars.

Verlander got his 200th postseason strikeout when he fanned Victor Robles for the second out in the second inning. The eight-time All-Star passed John Smoltz, who had 199 and was in the TV booth for Fox to see his record fall.

Verlander and Strasburg both settled in after their early wobbles and neither pitcher allowed the hitters to string much together until things fell apart for Houston in the seventh.

Suzuki sent Verlander's 100th pitch sailing above the seats in left field to start the inning and put the Nationals on top. Ryan Pressly, who left Game 6 of the ALCS with a knee injury, took over and didn't look right from the start.

He walked Turner before manager AJ Hinch called for his first intentional walk of the season when he gave Juan Soto a free pass to load the bases with two outs. Howie Kendrick, Asdrúbal Cabrera and Zimmerman followed with successive singles to bust this one open, putting the Nationals up 8-2.

"The inning spiraled out of control," Hinch said.

TOP: Asdrubal Cabrera catches a line drive by the Astros Yordan Alvarez during the second inning.
MATT SLOCUM/ AP PHOTO

RIGHT: Stephen Strasburg let out a yell after getting out of the sixth inning.
MATT SLOCUM / AP PHOTO

FAR RIGHT: Adam Eaton, left, celebrates his two-run home run with Victor Robles, right, during the eighth inning.
MATT SLOCUM / AP PHOTO

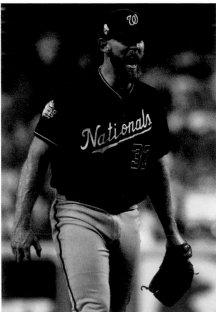

TOP LEFT: Kurt Suzuki watches as the ball leaves the park for a home run during the seventh inning.
DAVID J. PHILLIP / AP PHOTO

LOWER LEFT: Asdrubal Cabrera come through with a base hit driving in two runs.
DAVID J. PHILLIP / AP PHOTO

TOP RIGHT: Jose Altuve, right, is tagged out at third by Anthony Rendon after trying to steal during the first inning.
MATT SLOCUM / AP PHOTO

LOWER RIGHT: Catcher Kurt Suzuki and relief pitcher Javy Guerra celebrate the win.
DAVID J. PHILLIP / AP PHOTO

Astros Spoil World Series Return to D.C.

WASHINGTON — From the moment George Springer jumped on the game's third pitch for a single, then quickly swiped a base, to the way he and his teammates sprinted off the field after the final out a little past midnight Saturday, the Houston Astros were suddenly aggressive and energetic.

And suddenly right back in the thick of this World Series.

Yes, the Fall Classic finally showed up back in Washington, 86 years later -- and, sparked by Springer and Jose Altuve, the Astros finally showed up in the Fall Classic.

Springer had two of Houston's four steals, Altuve doubled twice before scoring each time, Zack Greinke repeatedly worked out of trouble, and the Astros made sure they wouldn't go quietly despite looking listless twice at home, beating the Nationals 4-1 to cut their Series deficit to 2-1.

"We're pretty good, too," Astros manager AJ Hinch said. "It kind of re-establishes us."

"We didn't panic," Altuve said.

Washington's eight-game winning streak, tied for the longest in a single postseason, ended with a sloppy performance in the first Series game hosted by the nation's capital since the Senators lost to the New York Giants in 1933.

A sellout crowd of 43,867, dressed mostly in red for the occasion, soaked it all in, standing in unison at key moments, booing ball-strike calls that hurt their team, chanting "Let's go, Nats!" often and even getting to do their "Baby Shark" sing-and-clap-along when that children's tune blared as a walk-up song in the sixth.

"It was electric," Nationals manager Dave Martinez said. "The boys in the dugout, they were fired up."

But the wild-card Nationals were unable to move one win from a championship, undone by an inability to come through in the clutch: Birthday boy Juan Soto, MVP candidate Anthony Rendon and Co. were 0 for 10 with runners in scoring position, leaving 12 runners on base.

"Tonight we were a little bit aggressive outside the strike zone," Martinez said. "We took balls I thought we should hit, uncharacteristic of what we've been doing. Greinke got out of some jams. [We] got opportunities early. We couldn't capitalize."

How big was this win for Houston?

No team ever has come back after dropping the first three games of a World Series.

"Not the script you'd want to write to start out a World Series," said reliever Will Harris, who retired all five batters he faced. "We believe in each other in there. We know we have obviously a very talented, capable team."

That's why several Astros players gathered for a private meeting following their 12-3 Game 2 loss.

"Some guys said some things that a lot of us maybe were thinking in our head, but it's sometimes nice to hear them out loud," Harris said.

After playing what might have been their worst baseball of 2019, the Astros played like the club that led the majors with 107 regular-season wins.

And, not surprisingly, Altuve was in the middle of a lot of it. He doubled in the third and fifth, coming home on singles by Michael Brantley.

"Jose's the heart and soul of what we do," Hinch said. "It was his turn to be a catalyst."

Greinke allowed seven hits and three walks in 4 2/3 innings, but managed to

yield just one run. He was followed by five relievers who combined to give up two hits and zero runs the rest of the way.

Josh James earned the win, striking out Ryan Zimmerman with two aboard to end the fifth.

Roberto Osuna heard boos when he entered in the ninth, then got three outs for a save.

Josh Reddick delivered an RBI single in the second, Robinson Chirinos homered off the foul-pole screen in the sixth and Houston scored four runs in 5 1/3 innings off Anibal Sanchez. The 35-year-old righty had taken a no-hitter into the eighth inning of his previous start. Springer got to him right away.

Sanchez went sprawling off the mound to try to make a play, but couldn't. All part of a rough night in which he got so upset by a couple of ball calls that he asked plate umpire Gary Cederstrom, "Where was that one?"

Sanchez also barely avoided taking a ball to the face, getting his glove in the way just in time. Another Houston hit came when Springer sent a comebacker off reliever Joe Ross' foot.

In sum: After the Nationals could do no wrong for so long, things went awry.

They made two errors and at least three other misplays on what were ruled hits. Washington catcher Kurt Suzuki left in the sixth with a right hip flexor problem. Soto, serenaded by fans in left field to celebrate his 21st birthday, was charged with an error for a wild throw home, let another ball trickle past his glove and went 0 for 4 with three strikeouts at the plate.

He went down looking to end the game.

"Nobody," Washington outfielder Adam Eaton said, "thought this was going to be easy."

ABOVE: Fans do the baby shark as Gerardo Parra bats during the sixth inning.
PATRICK SEMANSKY / AP PHOTO

RIGHT: The Astros Yuli Gurriel nearly hits pitcher Anibal Sanchez with a line drive in the fifth inning.
ALEX BRANDON / AP PHOTO

LEFT: Victor Robles makes a great catch on a deep drive by the Astros Jose Altuve during the first inning.
JEFF ROBERSON / AP PHOTO

TOP: The Astros Josh Reddick shares a laugh with Anthony Rendon during a break in the action.
JEFF ROBERSON / AP PHOTO

LOWER: Adam Eaton makes the catch on a sinking line drive during the sixth inning.
JEFF ROBERSON / AP PHOTO

Astros Tie Series 2-2

WASHINGTON — Not bad for a TBA.

Unheralded rookie José Urquidy outpitched all those big-name aces who preceded him, quieting Washington's bats and the Nationals Park crowd, too.

Alex Bregman busted out of his slump with a go-ahead single in the first inning and a grand slam in the seventh, and the resurgent Houston Astros routed the Nationals 8-1 to pull even at two games apiece in an unpredictable World Series that's been one big road show.

Urquidy had never pitched above Class A before this year. This stage seemed surreal.

"A couple of moments," he said, "I was thinking about, oh my God, I'm in a World Series pitching."

Visiting teams have won the first four games for the first time since 1996.

"This is what it's all about," Bregman said. "This is a beautiful thing. It's two teams battling it out. They've got great pitching, great offenses. It's been fun so far, and just want to keep it rolling."

Yuli Gurriel also drove in a run in the first as Houston strung together four singles in a seven-pitch span for a 2-0 lead against Patrick Corbin. Robinson Chirinos homered for the second straight day, a two-run drive that boosted the lead to 4-0 in the fourth.

Fans started leaving in the seventh, when the Astros sent 10 batters to the plate and battered the bullpen. Bregman had the big blow, driving a low, inside fastball from Fernando Rodney into the left field stands of the ballpark where he was the All-Star Game MVP in 2018.

Bregman held his bat high as he slowly walked out of the batter's box, then took 28 seconds to savor circling the bases.

Orange-clad Houston fans in the right field upper deck chanted "Let's go Astros!" as Nationals fans were silenced. Wild-card Washington lost consecutive games for the first time since Sept. 13-14 against Atlanta.

Starting pitchers were the talk of the Series coming in, with Washington's Stephen Strasburg, Scherzer and Corbin combining for 12 All-Star picks and three Cy Young Awards. The baseball cards of Houston's Cole, Justin Verlander and Zack Greinke sparkle with 17 All-Star selections, two Cy Youngs and one MVP.

But there were just five 1-2-3 innings by starters in the first three games, and the most consecutive outs were turned in by Nationals veteran Aníbal Sánchez, who retired seven straight in Game 3.

Urquidy exceeded them all.

"Maybe he doesn't have the Max Scherzer, Gerrit Cole name, but he's got good stuff," Washington leadoff man Trea Turner said.

Urquidy wasn't even announced as Houston's starter until after Game 3, with manager AJ Hinch hoping to piece together innings any way he could.

Urquidy allowed two hits in five scoreless innings, striking out four and walking none.

"From the very beginning I thought he was calm, I thought he was in control of his stuff," Hinch said. "His fastball had a little extra life to it. And then he just came up with big pitch after big pitch."

Mixing four-seam fastballs in the mid-90 mph range with two-seamers, sliders, curves and changeups, Urquidy set down the Nationals in order in the second, fourth and fifth, retiring his final nine batters. He threw 30 of his first 38 pitches for strikes, 45 of 67 overall.

"He flipped his percentages," Washington's Adam Eaton said. "He threw me three

OPPOSITE: Houston first baseman Yuli Gurriel, right, just beats Trea Turner to the bag to get the out.
JEFF ROBERSON / AP PHOTO

sliders my first at-bat — and he throws it like 10% of the time. So I was just like, going back, scratching my noggin."

Josh James, Will Harris, Héctor Rondón, Brad Peacock and Chris Devenski combined for two-hit relief to close it out for Houston.

Washington's best chance to get back into the game came in the sixth, when Harris relieved with two on and one out and Houston ahead 4-0. Anthony Rendon singled off the pitcher's leg, loading the bases, and Juan Soto drove in a run with a groundout. Harris then struck out Howie Kendrick.

After going 7 for 21 with runners in scoring position during the first two games, the Nationals are 1 for 19 in the last two.

Chirinos, who homered off the screen on the left field foul pole to drive in Houston's final run in Game 3, sent a flat changeup from Corbin deep into the left field seats, then slapped his chest and grinned as he skipped across home plate. The catcher doubled in the ninth and is 4 for 11 against the Nationals.

Signed to a $140 million, six-year contract as a free agent last offseason, Corbin dropped to 1-3 in three postseason starts and four relief appearances. He actually lowered his ERA to 6.64.

Washington manager Dave Martinez was looking ahead.

"We've got two of our big horses going in the next two games," he said. "I just told the boys: 'Hey, we're in the World Series. We're going to play Game 5, tied 2-2. Who would have thought that in the beginning?'"

LEFT: Nats starter Patrick Corbin went six innings giving up four runs on seven hits.
JEFF ROBERSON / AP PHOTO

TOP: Members of the Nationals watch as the final out is made in Game 4.
PATRICK SEMANSKY / AP PHOTO

LOWER: Yan Gomes hits a double during the third inning.
PABLO MARTINEZ MONSIVAIS / AP PHOTO

Cole Dominates Nats

Astros take 3-2 Series lead

WASHINGTON — Gerrit Cole and the Houston Astros went to Washington, hoping to snap out of their funk and bring the World Series back to Minute Maid Park.

Not only are they heading home with more games to play, now they're just one win from another crown.

Handed the ball for what was supposed to be a high-stakes showdown against Max Scherzer, Cole gave Houston a firm grip on the Series by beating the Nationals 7-1 for a 3-2 lead.

Cole looked exactly like the stud who dominated baseball most of this season, bouncing back from a Game 1 clunker to pitch the Astros to their third straight win.

What a turnaround for his teammates, too — outscored 17-7 overall at home, Houston hammered the Nationals 19-3 in a Washington wipeout.

"We look like ourselves now," Astros manager AJ Hinch said.

Something was definitely missing for the Nationals. Namely, Scherzer.

The three-time Cy Young Award winner beat Cole in the opener, and was the Nats' best hope to slow Houston. But then Scherzer was scratched only 3 1/2

hours before game time because of an irritated nerve near his neck, an injury that could finish him for the Series.

Slumping rookie Yordan Álvarez and Carlos Correa each hit an early two-run homer off emergency starter Joe Ross. George Springer added another postseason drive for the Astros, who led the majors with a franchise-best 107 wins during the regular season.

"We actually hit some balls hard. We really did," Washington manager Dave Martinez said. "We just can't get nothing going these last three days."

With the road team winning every time so far, Houston heads home with two chances to claim its second title in three years. Justin Verlander gets the first try when he starts against Stephen Strasburg in Game 6.

Cole threw three-hit ball for seven innings, nicked only by Juan Soto's home run in the seventh, and struck out nine — eight on breaking balls.

Cole's mix of 99 mph heat and sharp secondary pitches induced a bevy of bad swings from the wild-card Nats as he improved to 4-1 with a 1.72 ERA this postseason. It might've been his final start for Houston — he's eligible for free agency and figures to command a steep price.

OPPOSITE: Juan Soto goes deep during the seventh inning.
ALEX BRANDON / AP PHOTO

Standing tall on the mound, Cole was unflappable in the face of 43,910 fans who went from fired up to furious to flat-out frustrated.

"He knew what this game meant to this Series," Hinch said. "So, nobody better to have on the mound."

The crowd gave Ross a huge ovation when he walked onto the field for warmups, sympathetic to his situation — he had pitched a total of two innings in almost a month.

The fans weren't finished, either.

Cole ended his outing by getting Victor Robles on a called third strike, a pitch the TV zone showed to be off the plate. Robles chucked his bat, helmet and gloves, and the crowd soon began a derisive chant at umpire Lance Barksdale.

"I know there were some choice words but that's just in the heat of the moment," Martinez said.

Cole acknowledged he finished his outing "with a break."

"It's tough. I think ultimately some of those pitches were off the plate," he said.

Most fans, meanwhile, stayed to the very end.

"They came to support us and really gave us everything they had all the way to the end, all 27 innings. Hats off to them. We apologize that we didn't give them more to celebrate," outfielder Adam Eaton said. "It wasn't that we didn't try."

Cole led the majors in strikeouts this year, was second to Verlander in wins and topped the AL in ERA. He took a 19-game winning streak into the opener but hardly looked like an October star, giving up five runs over seven uneven innings.

In his second shot at the Nationals, he aced the test. Cole escaped a first-and-third, no-out jam in the second, then breezed into the seventh.

With two outs and a full count on Ryan Zimmerman, Cole suddenly stepped off the mound — video that quickly made the rounds showed two women right behind the backstop lifting their tops to flash Cole. It wasn't clear whether he saw them, and he walked Zimmerman before getting Robles.

RIGHT: Tabbed as the starter just hours before the game Nats starting pitcher Joe Ross battled for five innings.
GEOFF BURKE / AP PHOTO

LEFT: Victor Robles throws his batting gloves in disgust after another questionable call by the home plate umpire during the seventh inning.
PABLO MARTINEZ MONSIVAIS / AP PHOTO

TOP: The Astros Carlos Correa hits a two-run home run during the fourth inning.
PABLO MARTINEZ MONSIVAIS / AP PHOTO

LOWER: Manager Dave Martinez yells at the home plate umpire as a number of questionable calls went against the Nats.
JEFF ROBERSON / AP PHOTO

115

Strasburg Pitches Nats in to Game 7 Showdown

HOUSTON — It's been an unconventional road to Game 7 of the World Series for Stephen Strasburg and the Washington Nationals.

Seizing the October spotlight he missed out on as a youngster, Strasburg pitched another postseason gem into the ninth inning as the Nationals beat the Houston Astros 7-2 to tie this Fall Classic at 3-3.

Juan Soto ran all the way to first base with his bat following a go-ahead homer, the same way Houston slugger Alex Bregman did earlier.

Yep, these wild-card Nationals have matched the heavily favored Astros swing for swing, hit for hit -- even home run celebration for home run celebration.

Now, it's onto a winner-take-all Game 7 to decide the only Series in which the visiting team won the first six.

"It's weird, really. You can't explain it," Washington manager Dave Martinez said.

Adam Eaton and Soto hit solo homers off Justin Verlander in the fifth to help the Nationals overcome a 2-1 deficit. Anthony Rendon also went deep and drove in five runs.

"Maybe they enjoy our park and maybe we enjoy their park," said Rendon, who attended high school 4 1/2 miles from Minute Maid Park. "We're not going to ask questions."

Fired up after a disputed call at first base went against them in the seventh, the Nationals padded their lead moments later when Rendon hit a two-run homer off Will Harris. Martinez, still enraged at umpires, was ejected during the seventh-inning stretch, screaming as a pair of his coaches held him back while the crowd sang along to "Deep in the Heart of Texas."

Rendon added a two-run double off Chris Devenski in the ninth to just about seal it after Strasburg gutted through without his best fastball to throw five-hit ball for 8 1/3 innings. Washington pitching coach Paul Menhart told Strasburg after the first that he was tipping pitches. Strasburg allowed only three more hits.

"Started shaking my glove, so they didn't know what I was throwing," Strasburg said. "It's something that has burned me in the past, and it burned me there in the first."

Strasburg was memorably shut down by the Nationals in September 2012 to protect his arm in his first full season following Tommy John surgery, and Washington was beaten by St. Louis in the Division Series.

He improved to 5-0 with a 1.98 ERA in six postseason outings this October -- five starts and one relief appearance -- despite failing to get a swing and miss in the first two innings for the first time this year. Eight of his nine swings and

OPPOSITE: Starting pitcher Stephen Strasburg is congratulated after being taken out of the game during the ninth inning of Game 6.
MATT SLOCUM / AP PHOTO

misses overall came on breaking balls, and Strasburg escaped a two-on, two-out jam in the fourth by striking out Carlos Correa.

After George Springer's one-out double put runners at second and third in the fifth, Jose Altuve struck out on a curve in the dirt and Michael Brantley hit a hard grounder to second.

"He has an uncanny ability to slow the game down when he's under any duress," Hinch said about Strasburg.

Sean Doolittle got the final two outs as the Nationals bullpen headed into Game 7 relatively rested.

Now the Nationals will attempt their ultimate comeback in a year when they were written off time after time, hoping for the first title in the 51-season history of a franchise that started as the Montreal Expos and the first for Washington since the Senators in 1924.

Visiting teams have won three straight Game 7s in the Series since the Cardinals defeated Texas at home in 2011.

"I don't think there's a person in the building that would have assumed that all road teams were going to win," Houston manager AJ Hinch said. "We've just got to make sure that last one is not the same."

Martinez's ejection came after Trea Turner was called out for interference when he ran on the fair side of the foul line and knocked the mitt off first baseman Yuli Gurriel in the seventh following his slow roller. Washington was leading 3-2 at the time and would have had runners on second and third with no outs.

RIGHT: Juan Soto hits a home during the fifth inning.
ERIC GAY / AP PHOTO

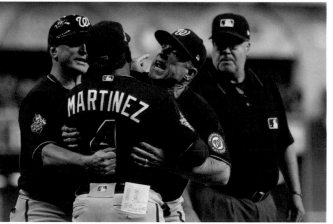

TOP: Trea Turner knocks the glove away from Astros' first basemanYuli Gurriel during the seventh inning. Turner was called out for runner interference on the play.
MATT SLOCUM / AP PHOTO

FAR LEFT: Anthony Rendon hits a two-run home run during the seventh inning.
ERIC GAY / AP PHOTO

LEFT: Manager Dave Martinez has to be restrained after being ejected for arguing an interference call during the seventh inning.
MATT SLOCUM / AP PHOTO

World Champions!

Nats rally to win franchise's first World Series

HOUSTON — Almost out of contention in May, champs in October.

Howie Kendrick, Anthony Rendon and the Washington Nationals completed their amazing comeback journey -- fittingly with one last late rally on the road.

In Game 7 of the World Series, no less.

Kendrick and Rendon homered in the seventh inning as the Nationals overcame a two-run deficit, rocking the Houston Astros 6-2 to win the first title in franchise history.

With all eyes on Max Scherzer and his remarkable recovery after a painkilling injection, these Nationals truly embraced their shot in the only Series where the road team won every game.

Even more against the odds: Juan Soto and Washington came from behind to win five elimination games this postseason, an unprecedented feat.

"What a story," said Ryan Zimmerman, the Nationals' initial draft pick back in 2005.

"I hope D.C.'s ready for us to come home!"

World Series MVP Stephen Strasburg, new lefty Patrick Corbin and the Nats brought the first World Series championship to the nation's capital since ol' Walter Johnson delivered the crown for the Senators in 1924.

But the incredible path these wild-card Nationals with the curly W logo took,

well, no one could have imagined.

"Resilient, relentless bunch of guys," manager Dave Martinez said. "They fought all year long."

Having lost star slugger Bryce Harper to free agency and beset by bullpen woes, Washington plummeted to 19-31 in late May. It got so bad there was talk around town the Nationals might fire Martinez and trade away Scherzer.

Instead, they stuck with the mantra that sprung up on T-shirts -- Stay In The Fight.

"That was out motto," Scherzer said.

And months later they finished it, indeed.

"Guess what? We stayed in the fight. We won the fight!" Martinez shouted during the trophy celebration on the field.

"We were down and out. We were 19-31. We didn't quit then, we weren't going to quit now," he said.

Washington kept pulling away after taking the lead, with Adam Eaton's two-run single in the ninth accounting for the final margin.

Zack Greinke was in complete control until Rendon -- a Houston prep and college star -- hit a home run that cut Houston's lead to 2-1 in the seventh.

When Soto followed with a one-out walk, manager AJ Hinch decided to make

Anthony Rendon gets the Nationals on the board with a seventh inning blast to left.
ERIC GAY / AP PHOTO

The clutch Howie Kendrick gives the Nationals the lead for good with a home run off the right field foul pole.
ERIC GAY / AP PHOTO

ABOVE: With two on and two out, Juan Soto makes a tough catch on a line drive by the Astros George Springer to end the second inning.
MATT SLOCUM / AP PHOTO

a move. He'd had ace starter Gerrit Cole warming up in the bullpen earlier, but this call was for Will Harris.

Kendrick connected on the second pitch, slicing a drive that hit the screen attached to the right field foul pole. Just like that, everything had changed for the team in orange that led the majors in wins, and the ballpark fell silent.

For Kendrick, another timely blow. At 36, playing on the oldest team in the majors, the journeyman earned the NL Championship Series MVP award against St. Louis after hitting the winning grand slam in the 10th inning of the deciding Game 5 in the Division Series at Dodger Stadium.

Then again, this was nothing new for the Nationals.

Washington rallied in the eighth to beat Milwaukee in the wild-card game and took the last two to beat Los Angeles in the NLDS, setting up a sweep of the Cardinals in the NLCS.

LEFT: Game 7 starter Max Scherzer plants a big kiss on the Commissioner's Trophy.
MATT SLOCUM / AP PHOTO

TOP: The Washington Nationals celebrate a World Series win.
SUE OGROCKI / AP PHOTO

LOWER: Anthony Rendon gets drenched as he celebrates with the Commissioner's Trophy and his teammates in the clubhouse.
DAVID J. PHILLIP / AP PHOTO

"The way this game went is the way our whole season went," said Zimmerman, the last player left from the 2005 Nationals team that debuted in Washington.

This World Series had lacked a lot of drama, but with Greinke and Scherzer grunting on every pitch, Game 7 was a classic duel from the start.

Yuli Gurriel put the Astros ahead with a home run in the second and Carlos Correa added an RBI single off Scherzer that made it 2-0 in the fifth.

Scherzer was done after the fifth, but he had done his job to keep it close. Only a few days earlier, the three-time Cy Young Award winner had been unable to lift his right arm because of nerve irritation near his neck.

Daniel Hudson, released by the Angels in March, closed it out for the Nationals, who made Houston pay for stranding so many runners on base all game. Hudson struck out Michael Brantley for the last out, then threw his glove to start the celebration.

RIGHT: Nationals manager Dave Martinez hugs the Commissioner's Trophy during the postgame celebration.
MATT SLOCUM / AP PHOTO

Pitchers

NAME, No.	POS	BAT	THW	AGE	HT	WT	BIRTH PLACE
Patrick Corbin, 46	SP	L	L	30	6' 3"	210 lbs	Clay, NY
Sean Doolittle. 63	RP	L	L	33	6' 2"	204 lbs	Rapid City, SD
Javy Guerra. 48	RP	R	R	33	6' 1"	216 lbs	Denton, TX
Daniel Hudson. 44	RP	R	R	32	6' 3"	225 lbs	Lynchburg, VA
Tanner Rainey. 21	RP	R	R	26	6' 2"	235 lbs	Folsom, LA
Fernando Rodney. 56	RP	R	R	42	5' 11"	240 lbs	Santa Barbara de Samana, Dominican Republic
Joe Ross. 41	SP	R	R	26	6' 4"	220 lbs	Berkeley, CA
Anibal Sanchez. 19	SP	R	R	35	6' 0"	205 lbs	Maracay, Venezuela
Max Scherzer. 31	SP	R	R	35	6' 3"	215 lbs	St. Louis, MO
Stephen Strasburg. 37	SP	R	R	31	6' 5"	235 lbs	San Diego, CA
Wander Suero. 51	RP	R	R	28	6' 4"	211 lbs	San Jose de Ocoa, Dominican Republic

Catchers

NAME	POS	BAT	THW	AGE	HT	WT	BIRTH PLACE
Yan Gomes. 10	C	R	R	32	6' 2"	215 lbs	Sao Paulo, Brazil
Kurt Suzuki. 28	C	R	R	36	5' 11"	210 lbs	Wailuku, HI

Infielders

NAME	POS	BAT	THW	AGE	HT	WT	BIRTH PLACE
Matt Adams. 15	1B	L	R	31	6' 3"	245 lbs	Philipsburg, PA
Asdrubal Cabrera. 13	2B	B	R	33	6' 0"	205 lbs	Puerto la Cruz, Venezuela
Brian Dozier. 9	2B	R	R	32	5' 11"	200 lbs	Fulton, MS
Anthony Rendon. 6	3B	R	R	29	6' 1"	200 lbs	Houston, TX
Trea Turner. 7	SS	R	R	26	6' 2"	185 lbs	Boynton Beach, FL
Ryan Zimmerman. 11	1B	R	R	35	6' 3"	215 lbs	Washington, NC

Outfielders

NAME	POS	BAT	THW	AGE	HT	WT	BIRTH PLACE
Adam Eaton. 2	RF	L	L	30	5' 9"	176 lbs	Springfield, OH
Gerardo Parra. 88	CF	L	L	32	5' 11"	210 lbs	Santa Bárbara, Venezuela
Victor Robles. 16	CF	R	R	22	6' 0"	190 lbs	Santo Domingo, Dominican Republic
Juan Soto. 22	LF	L	L	21	6' 1"	185 lbs	Santo Domingo, Dominican Republic
Michael A. Taylor. 3	CF	R	R	28	6' 4"	212 lbs	Fort Lauderdale, FL

Designated Hitter

NAME	POS	BAT	THW	AGE	HT	WT	BIRTH PLACE
Howie Kendrick. 47	DH	R	R	36	5' 11"	220 lbs	Jacksonville, FL